LET'S GET WEIRD
AN ADULT COLORING BOOK
By Cody Knepper
@very_average_art

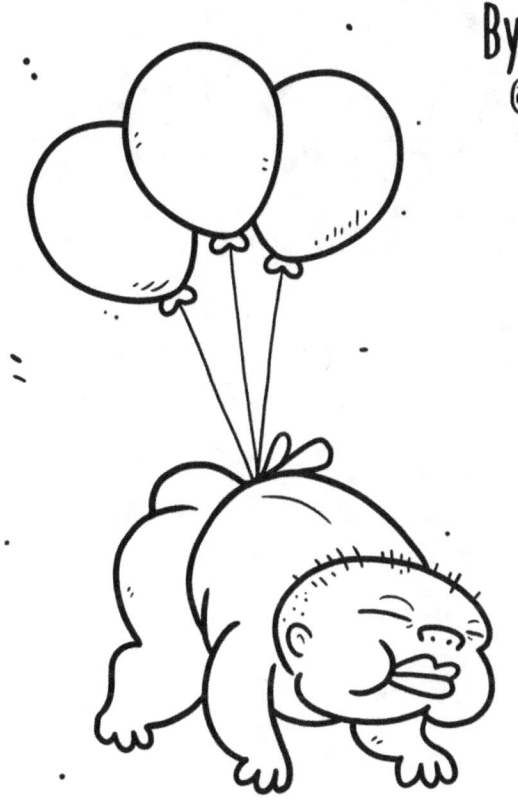
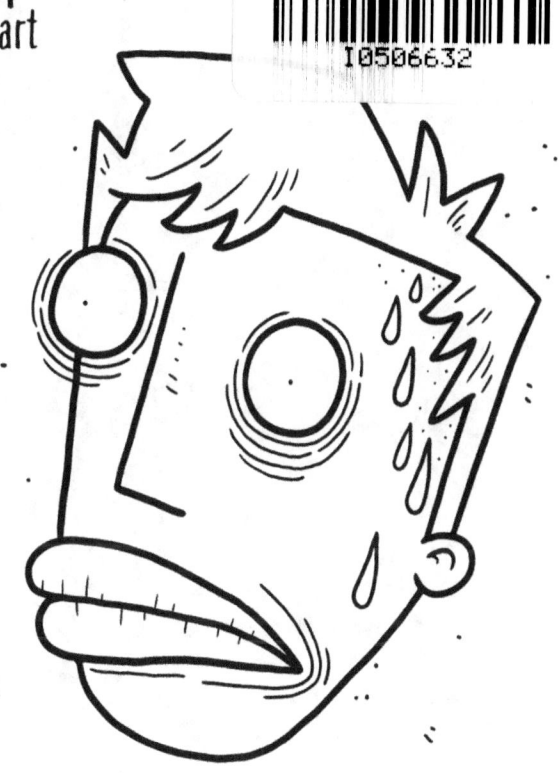

Copyright © Cody Knepper, 2020

ALL RIGHTS RESERVED. NO PART OF THIS BOOK MAY BE REPRODUCED IN ANY FORM BY ELECTRONIC OR MECHANICAL MEANS, INCLUDING INFORMATION STORAGE AND RETRIEVAL SYSTEMS, WITHOUT PERMISSION IN WRITING FROM THE PUBLISHER, EXCEPT BY A REVIEWER WHO MAY QUOTE BRIEF PASSAGES IN A REVIEW.

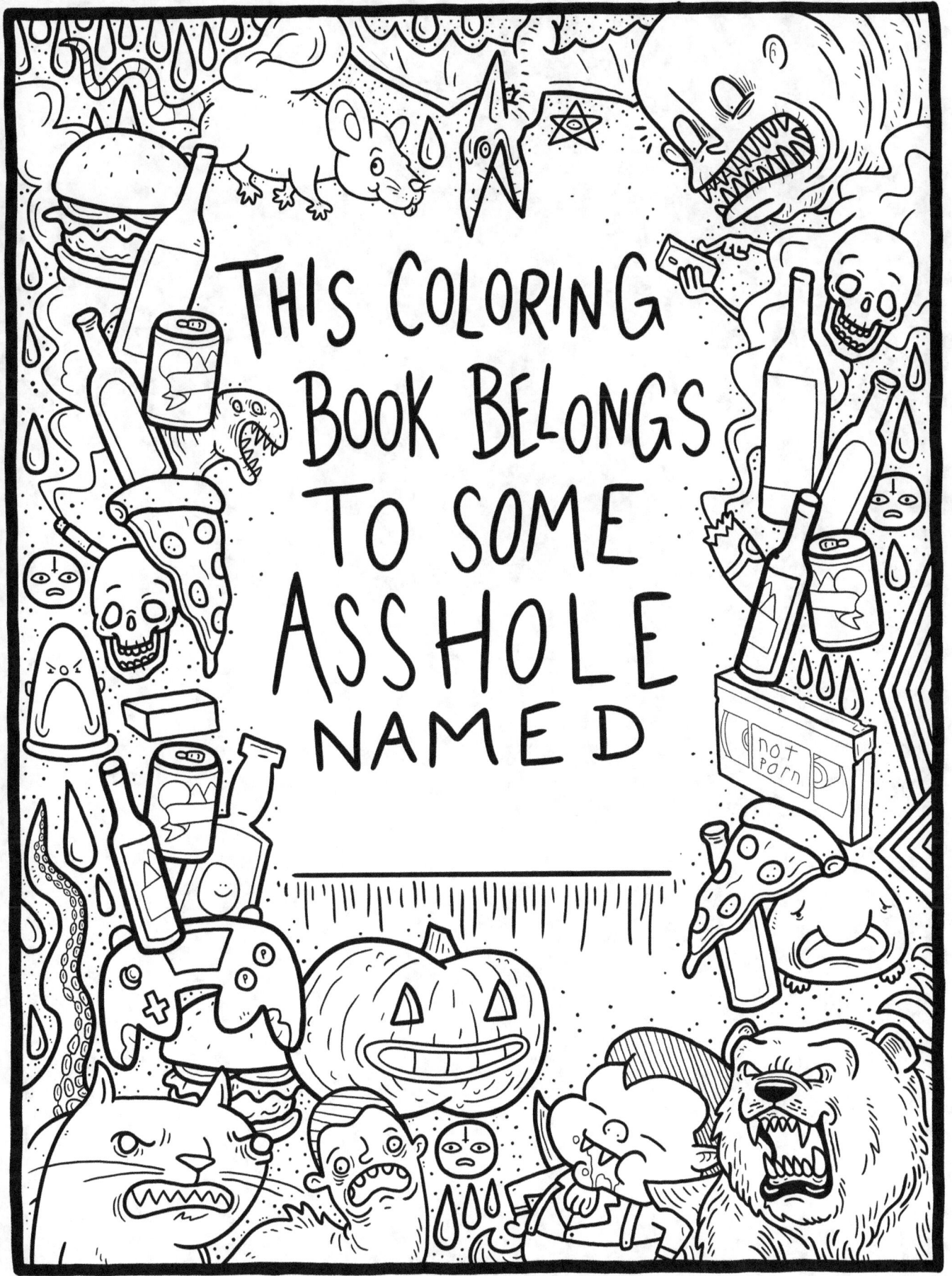

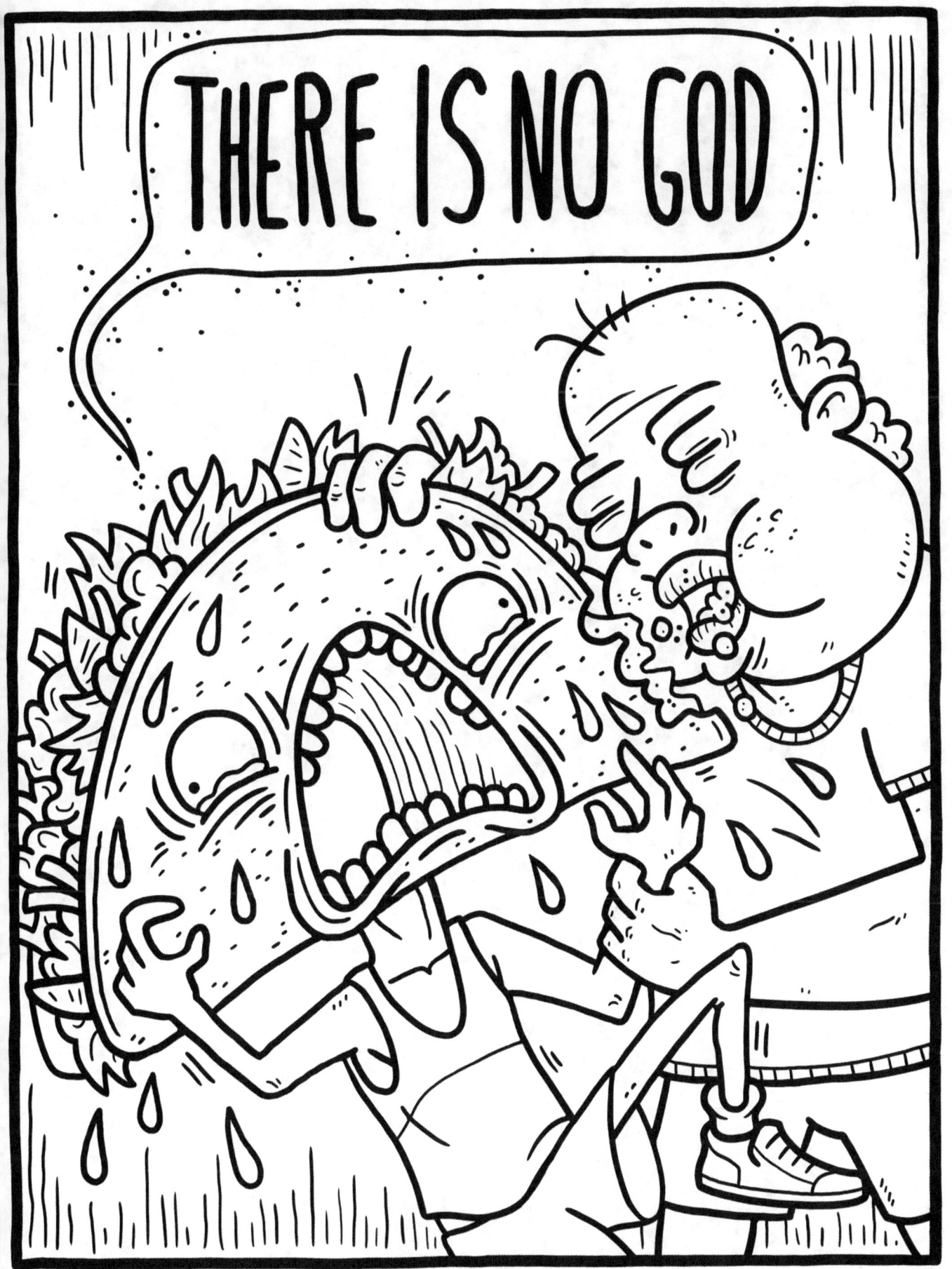

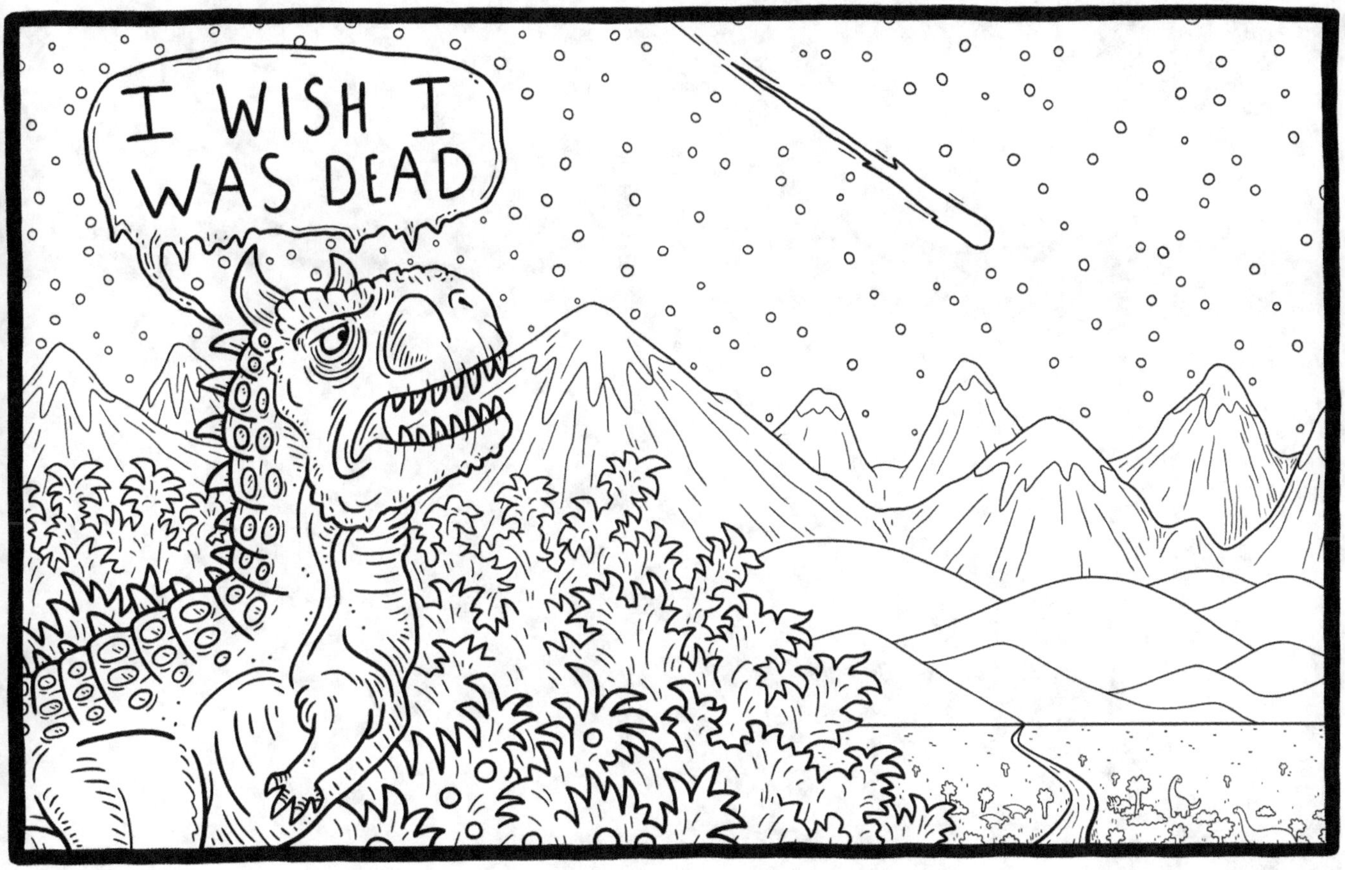

"I WISH I WAS DEAD"

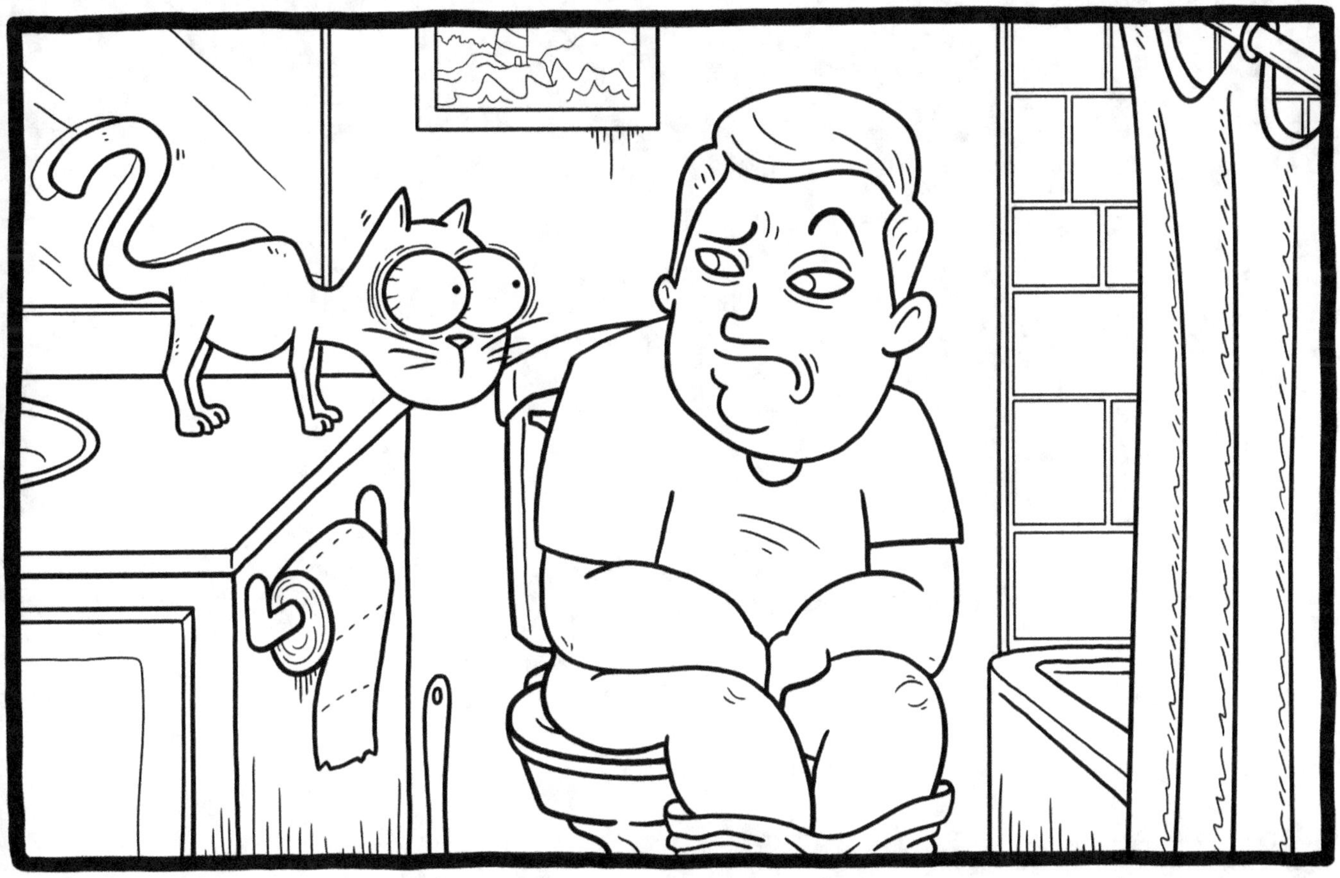

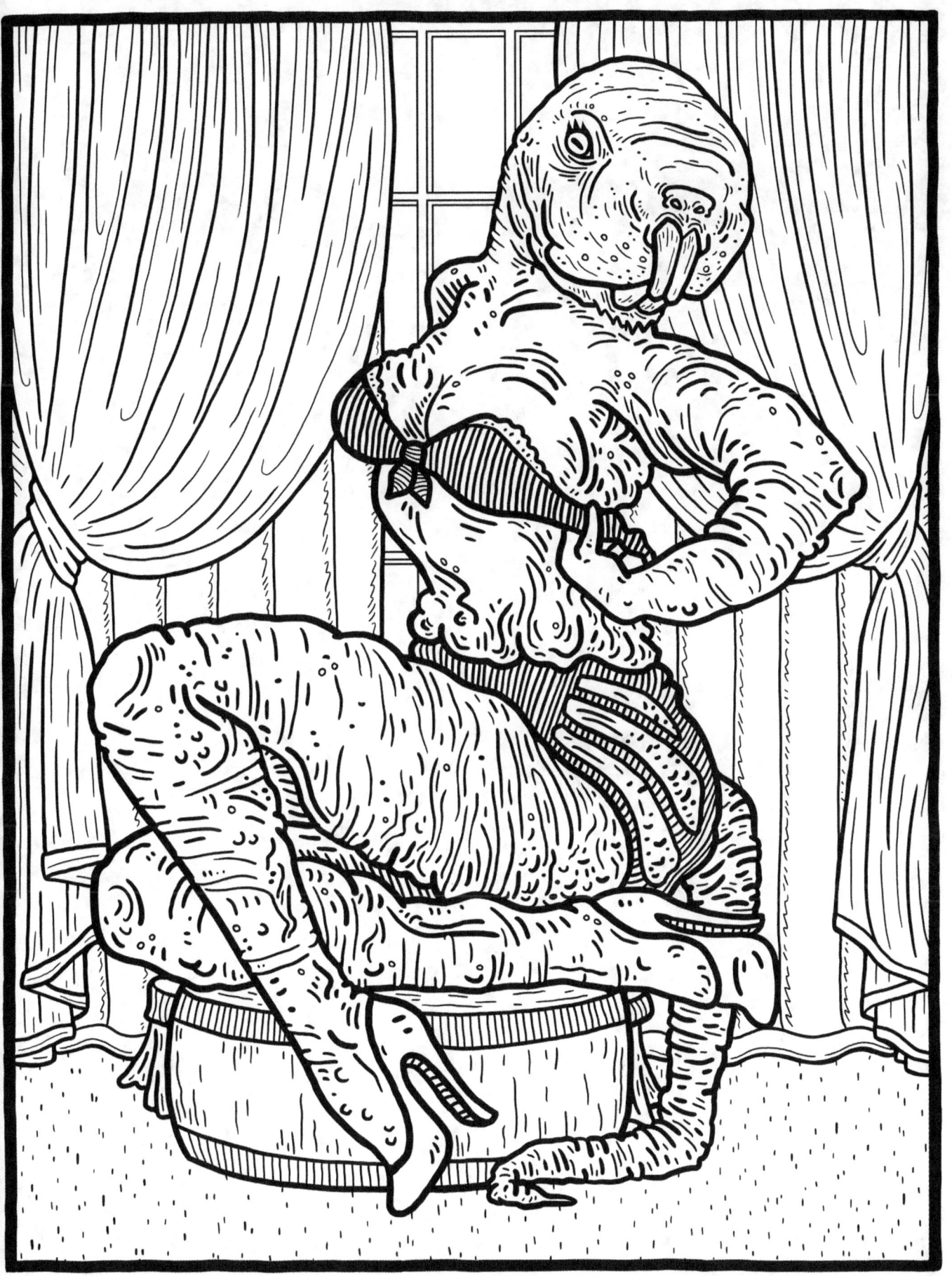

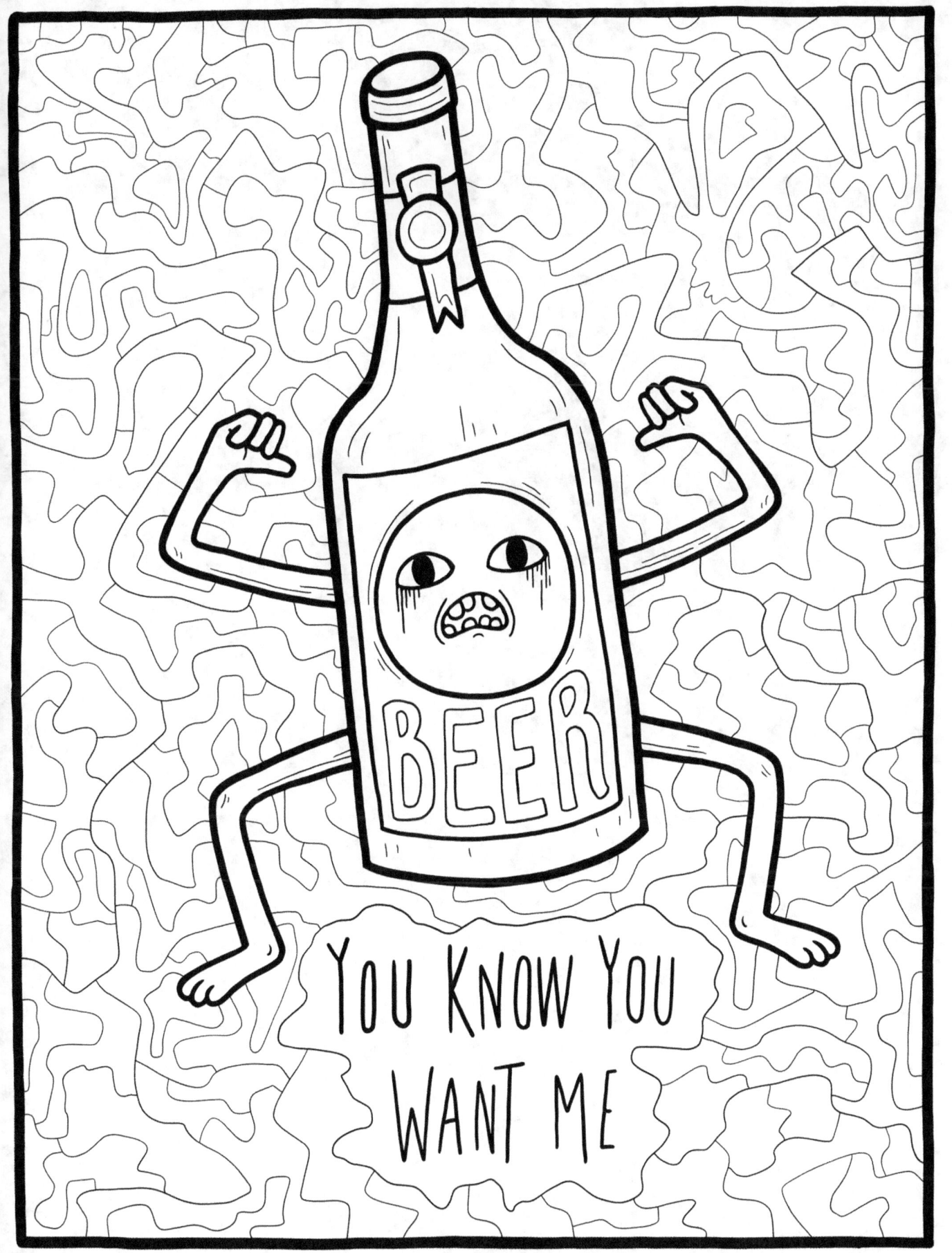

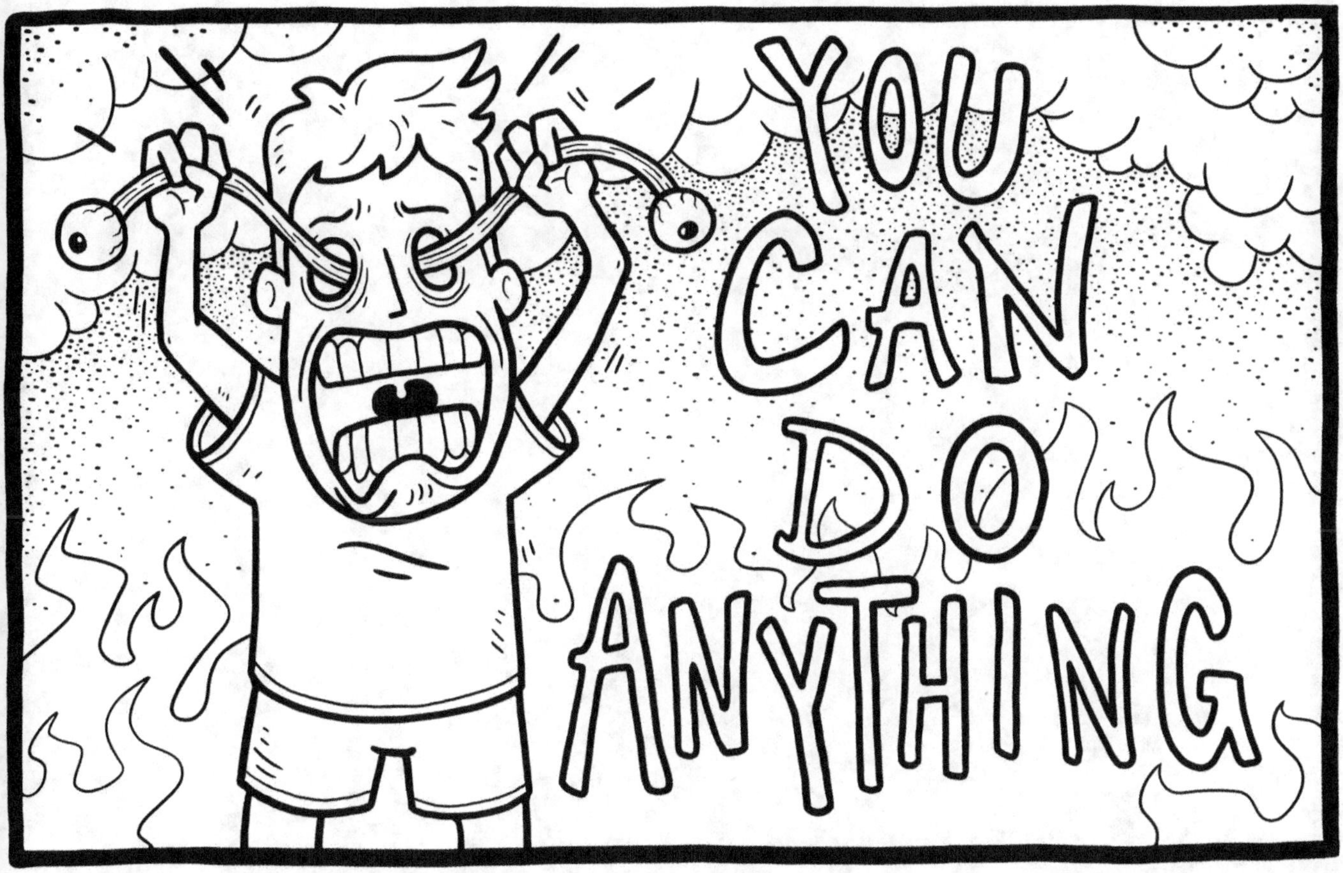

YOU CAN DO ANYTHING

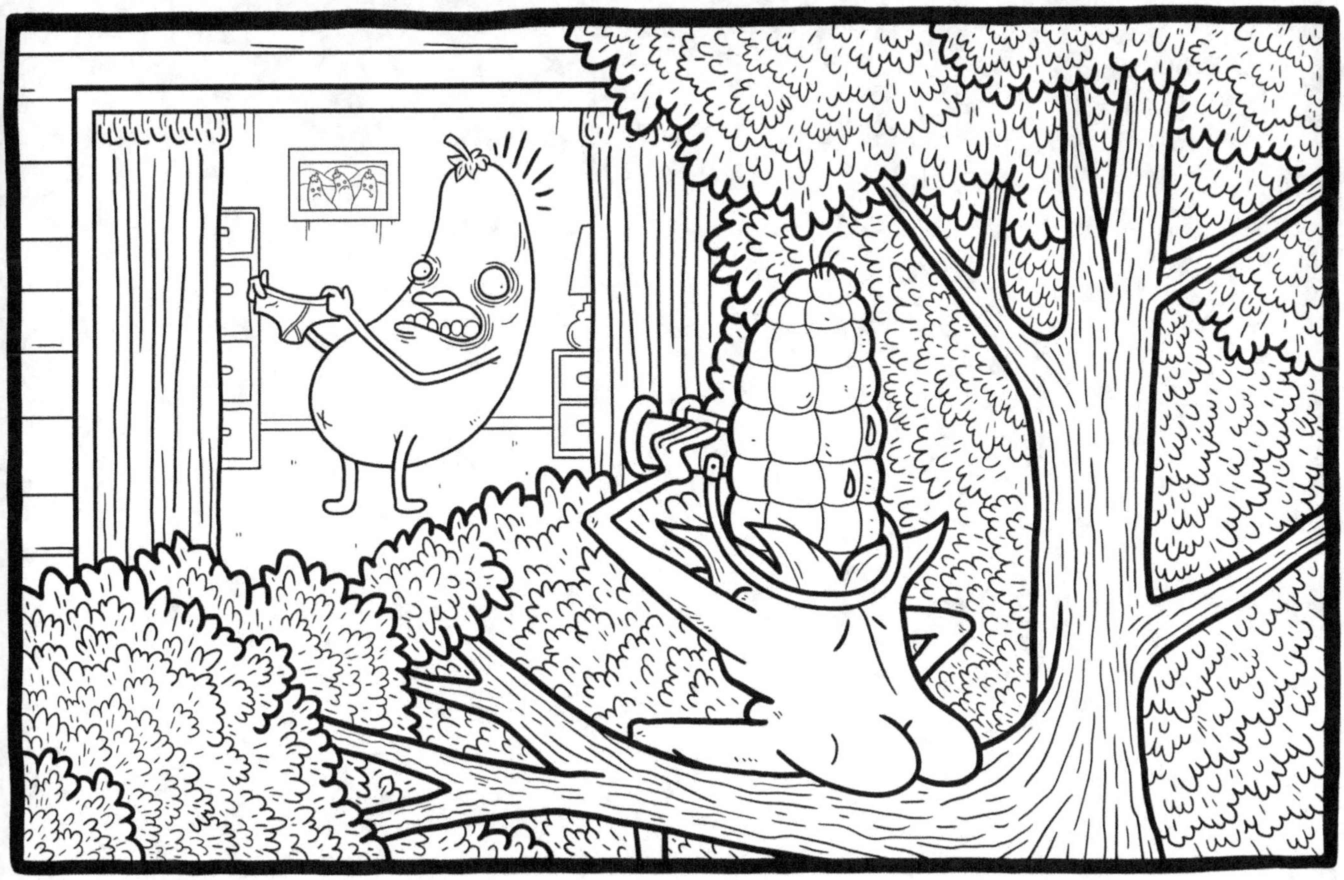

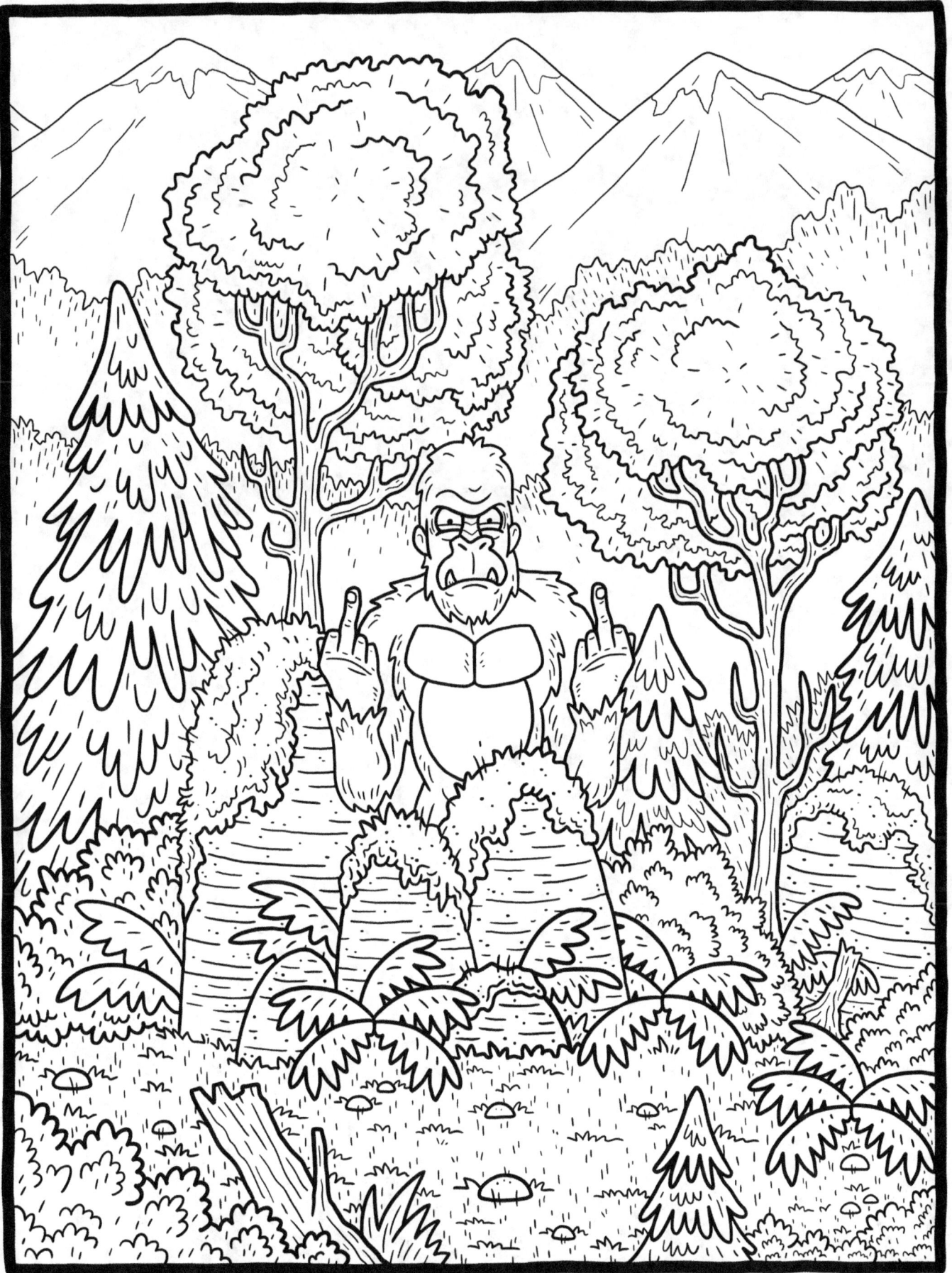

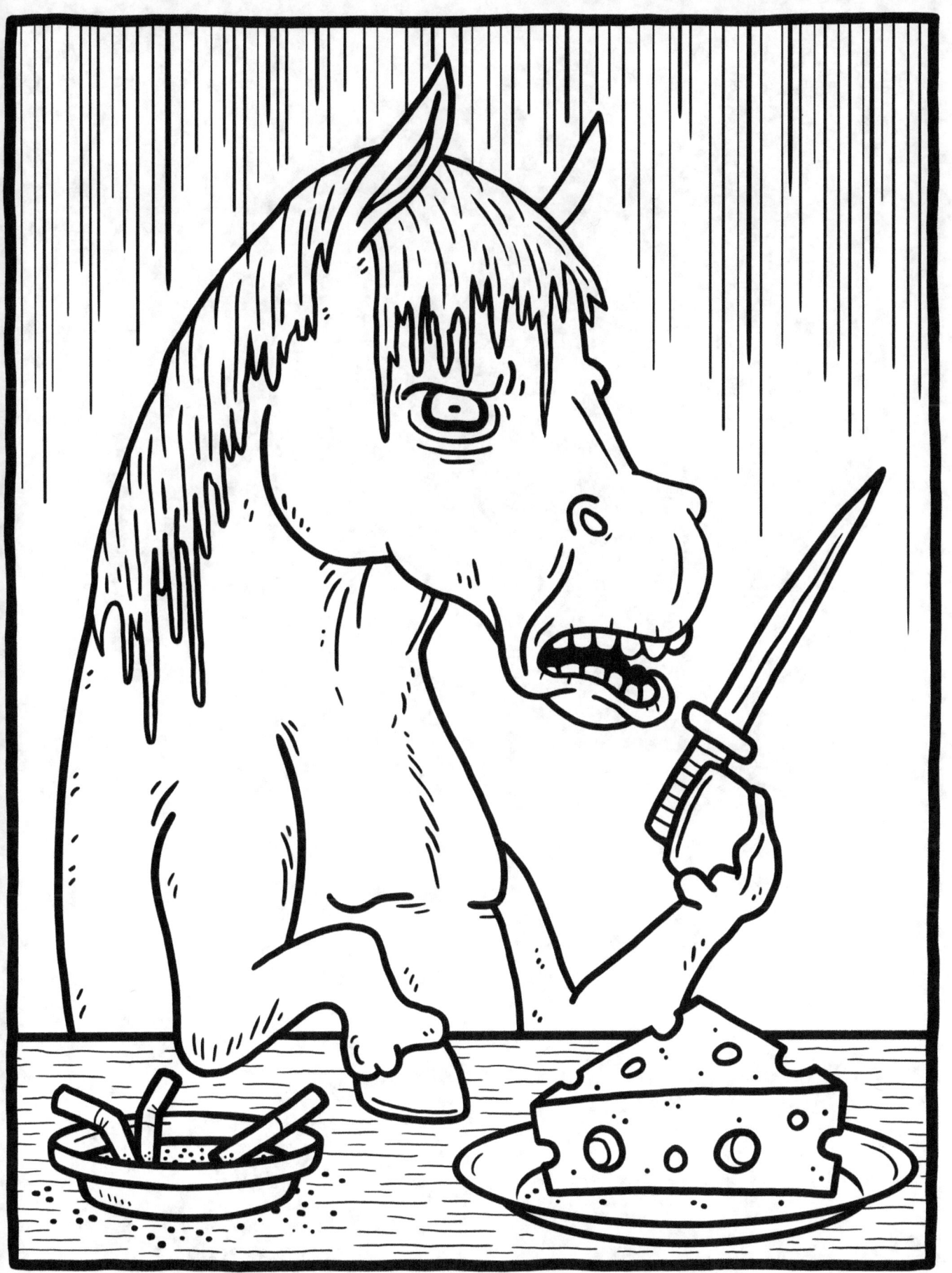

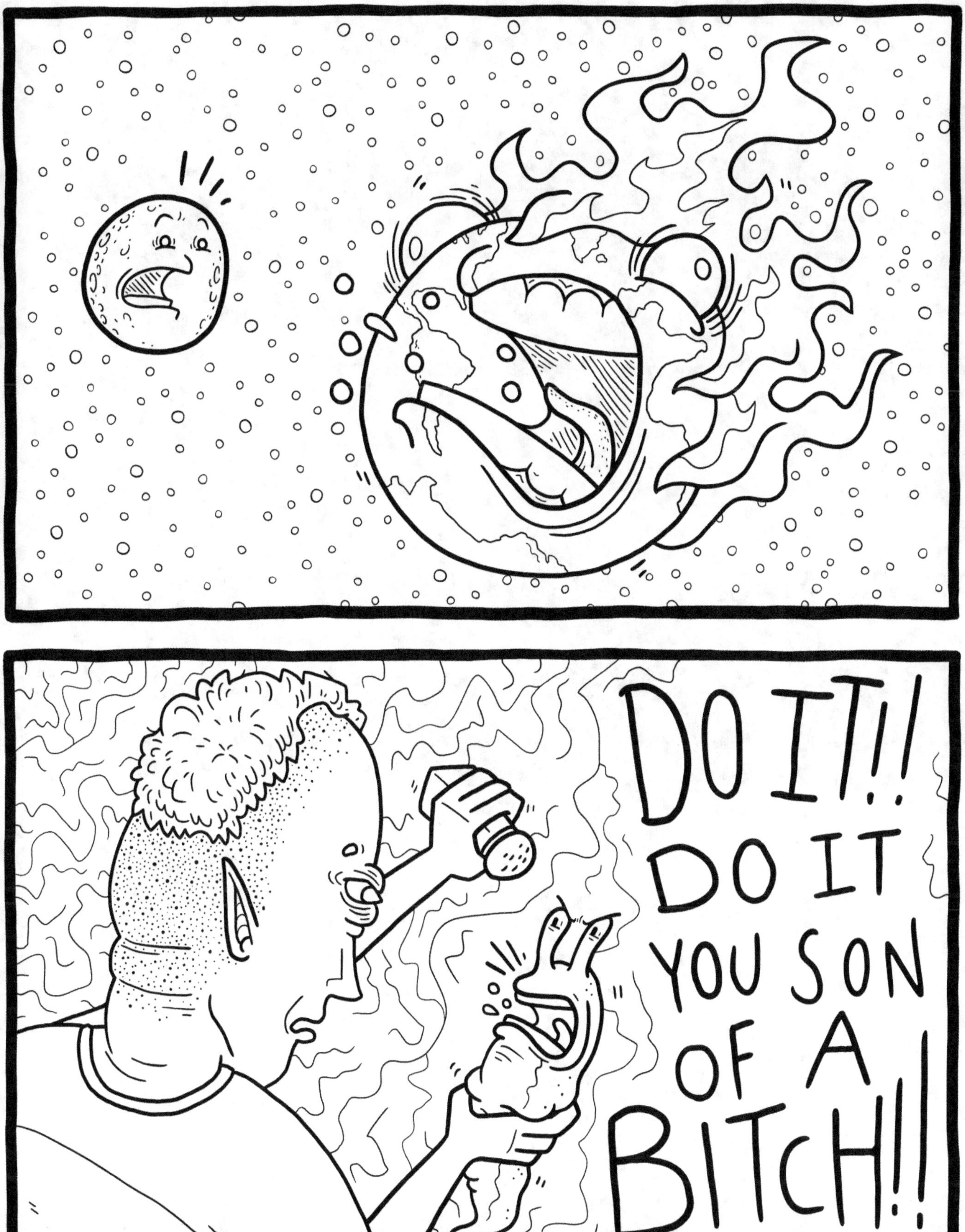

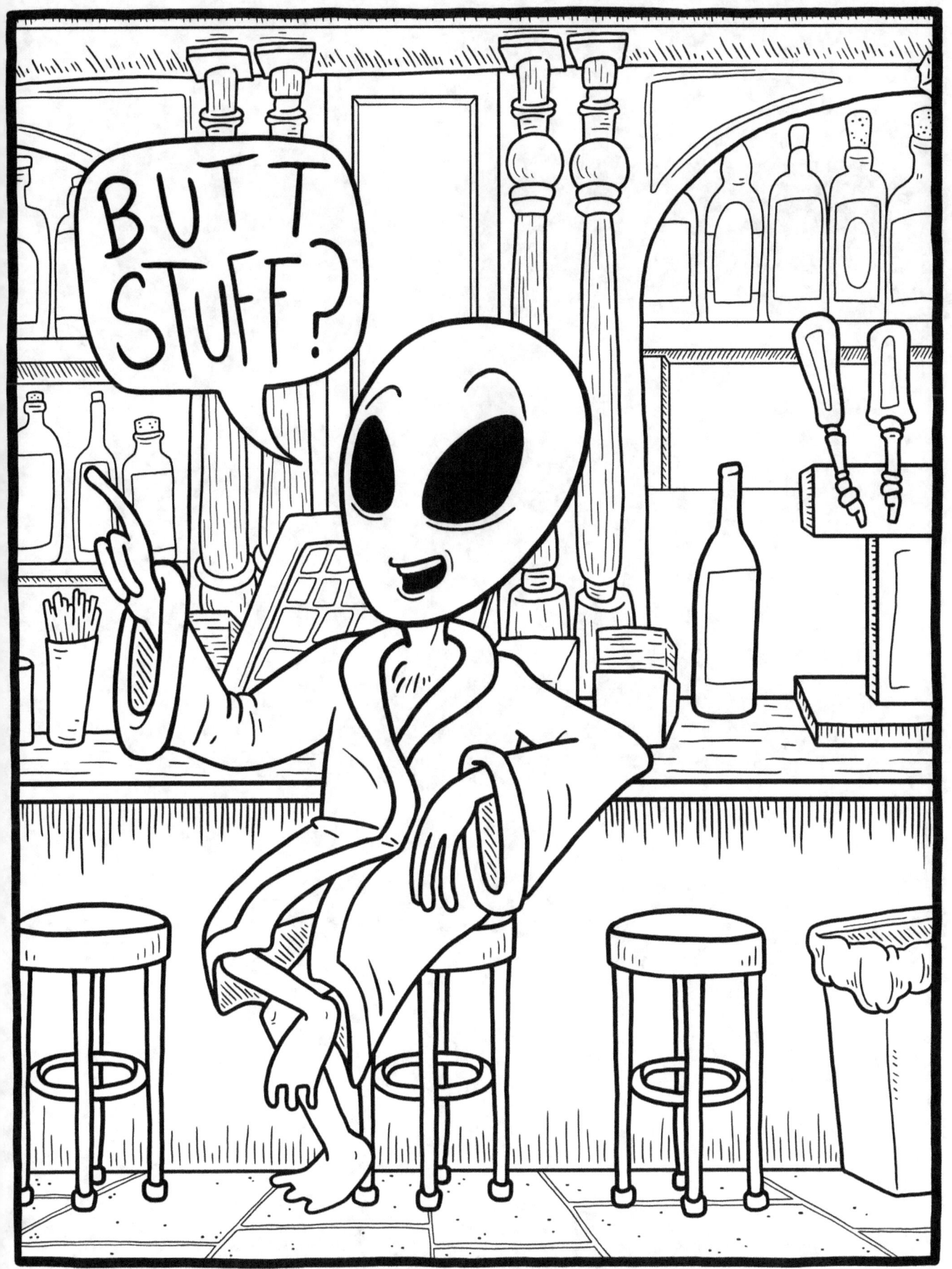

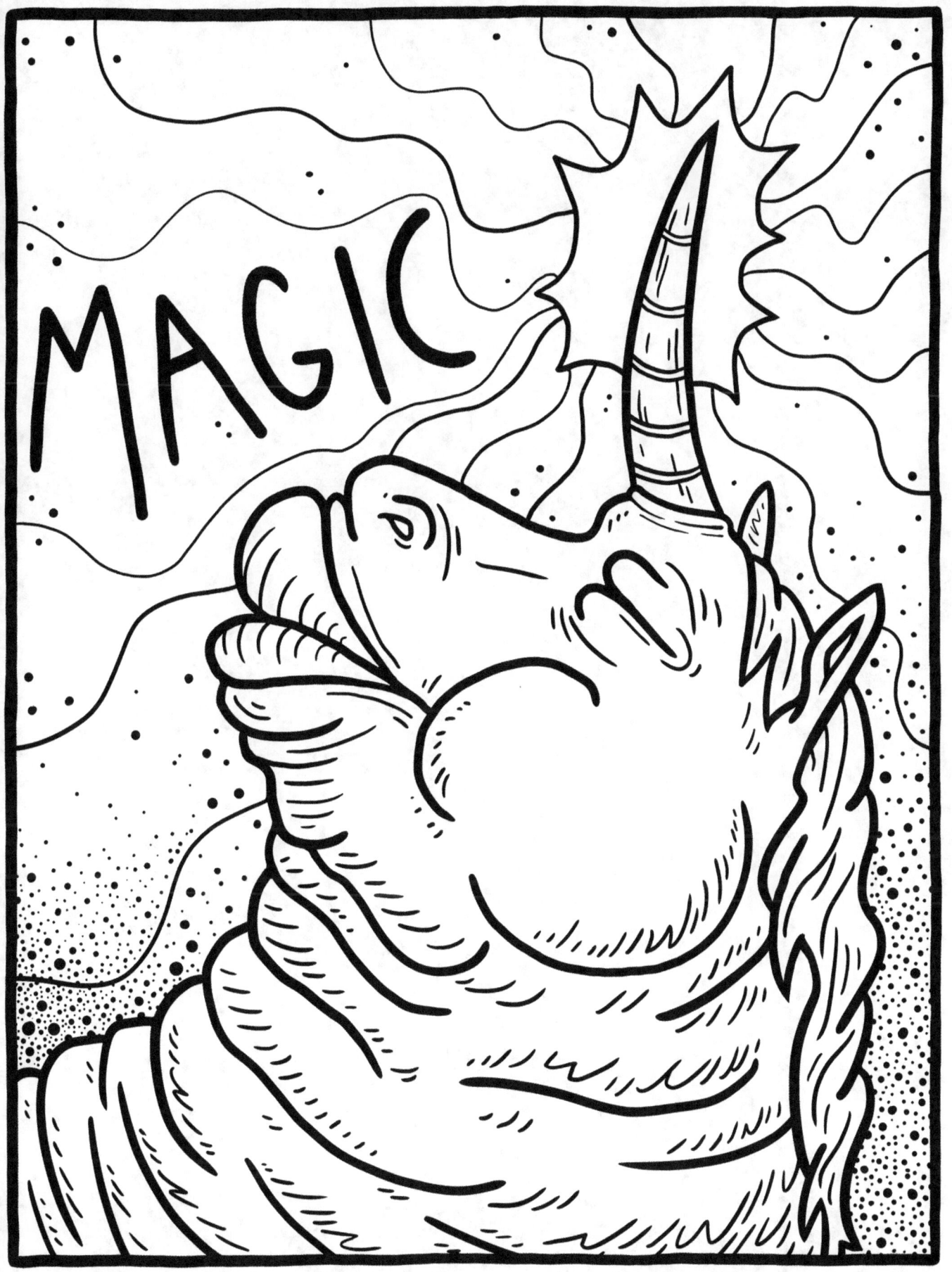

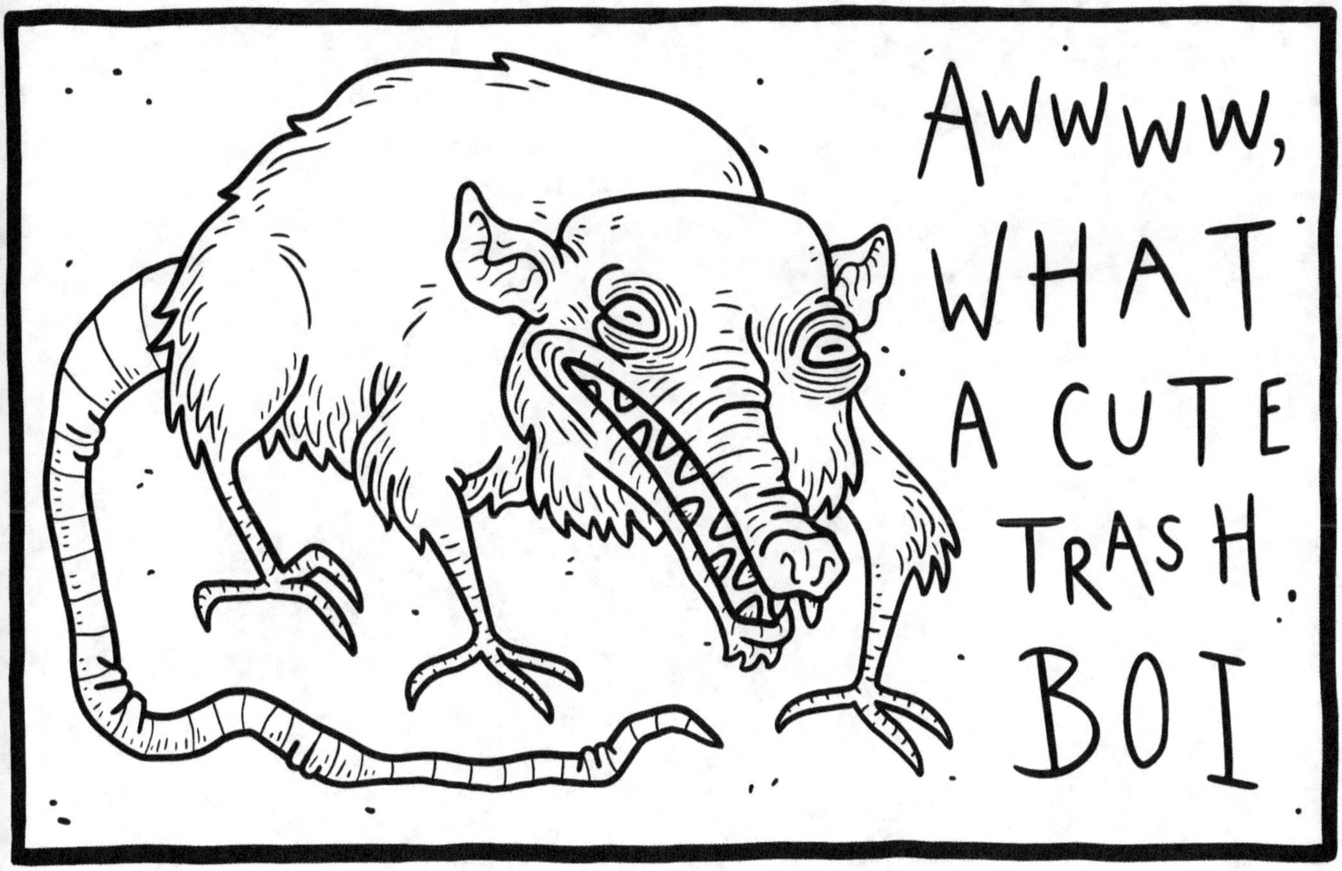

Awww, what a cute trash boi

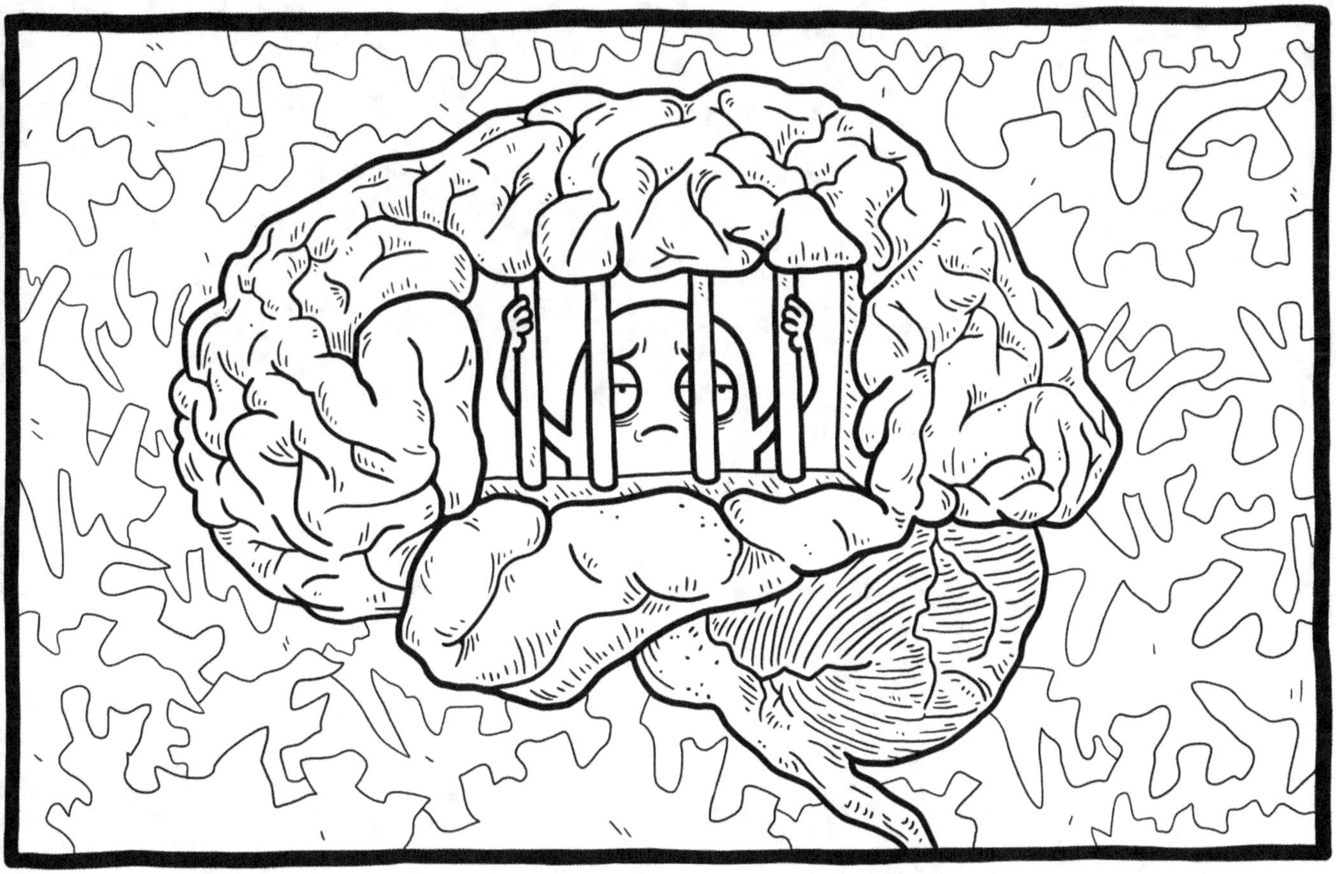

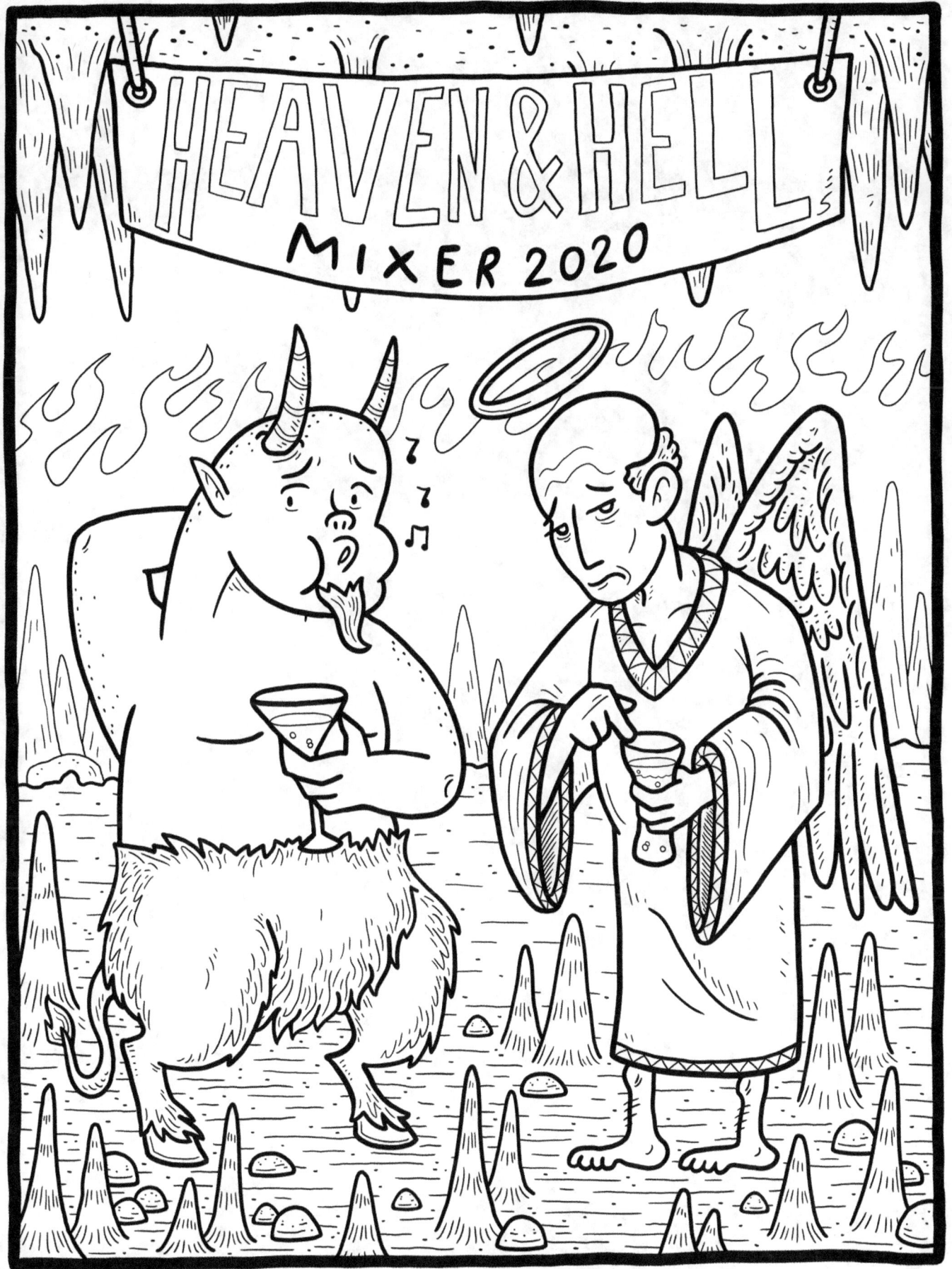

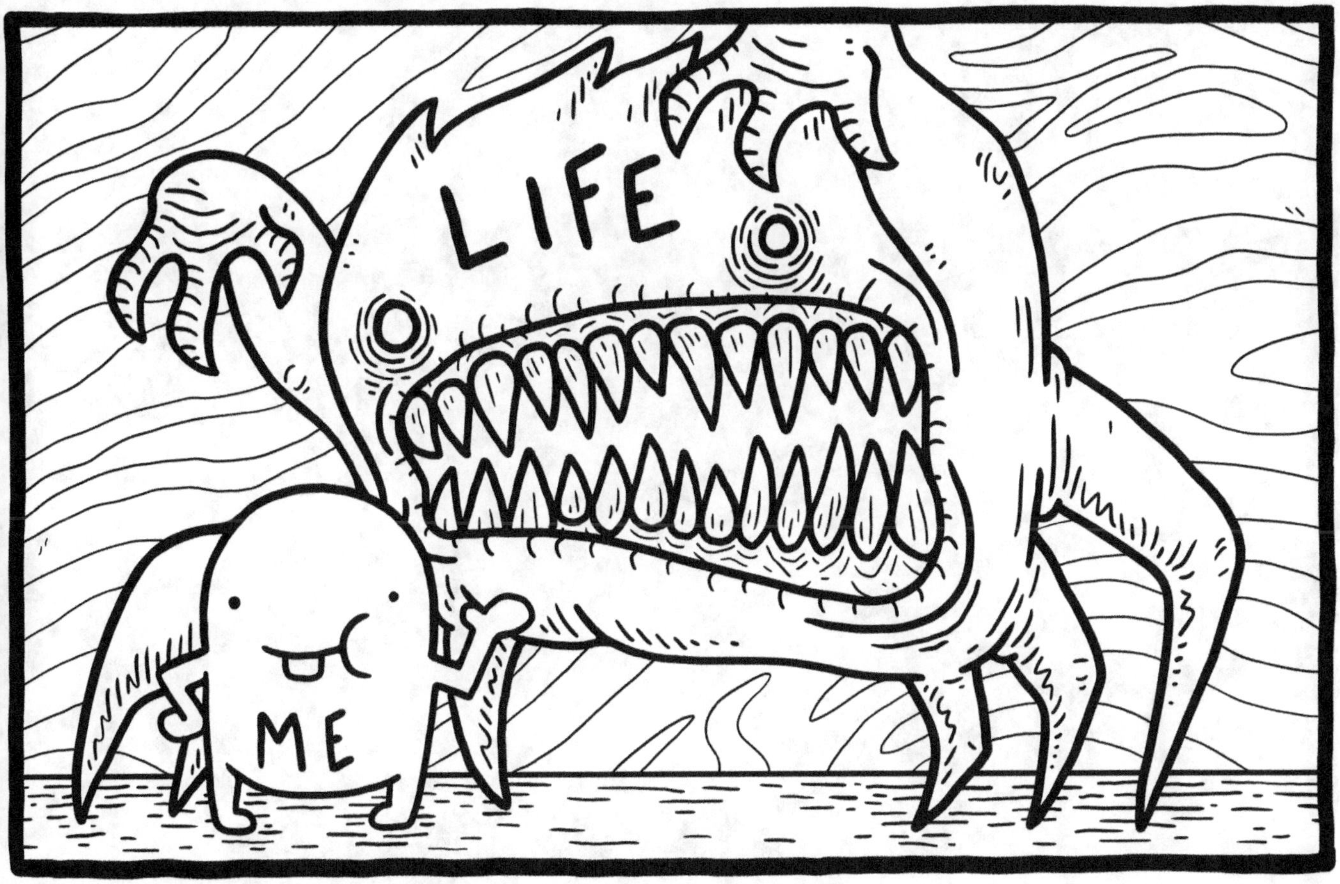

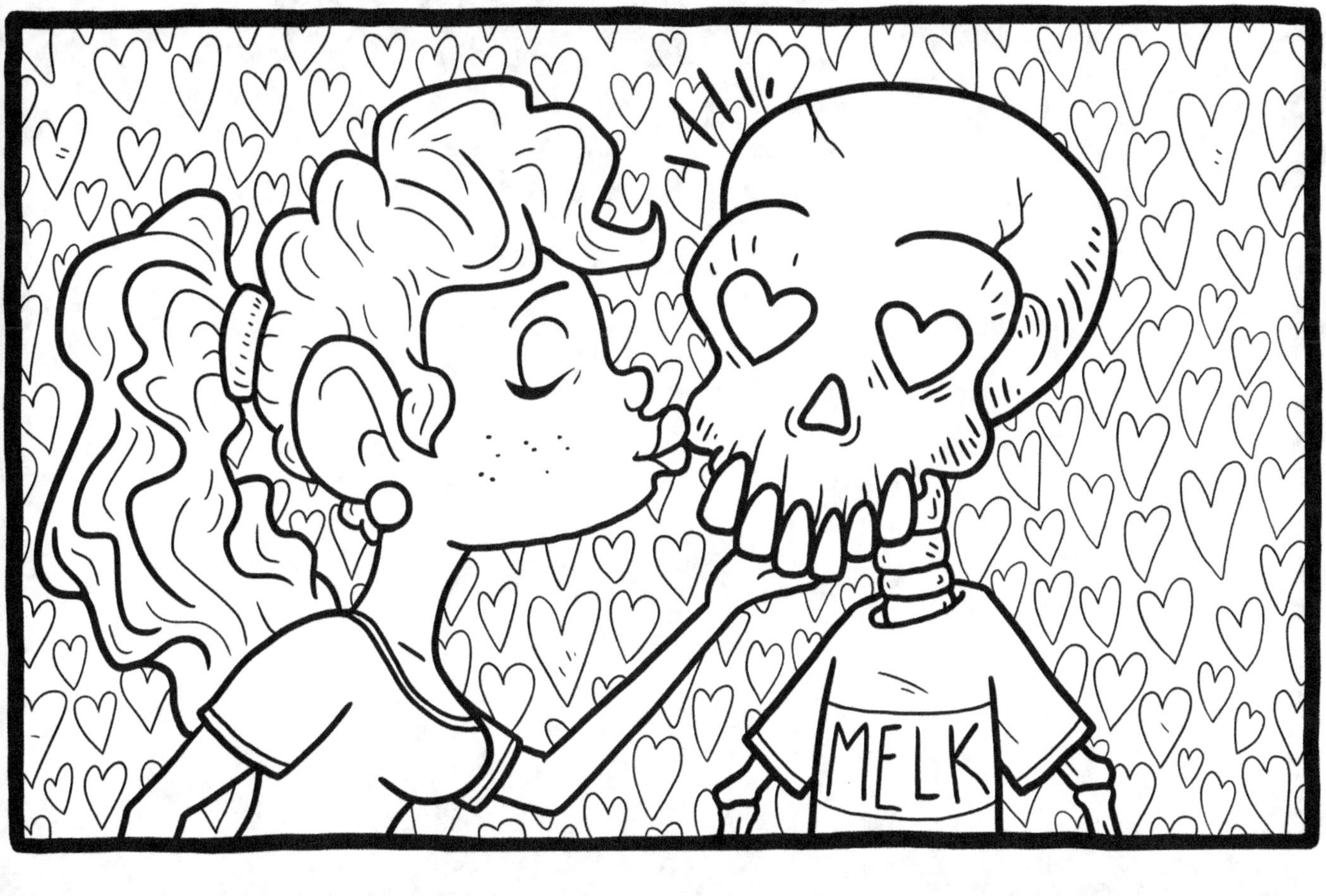

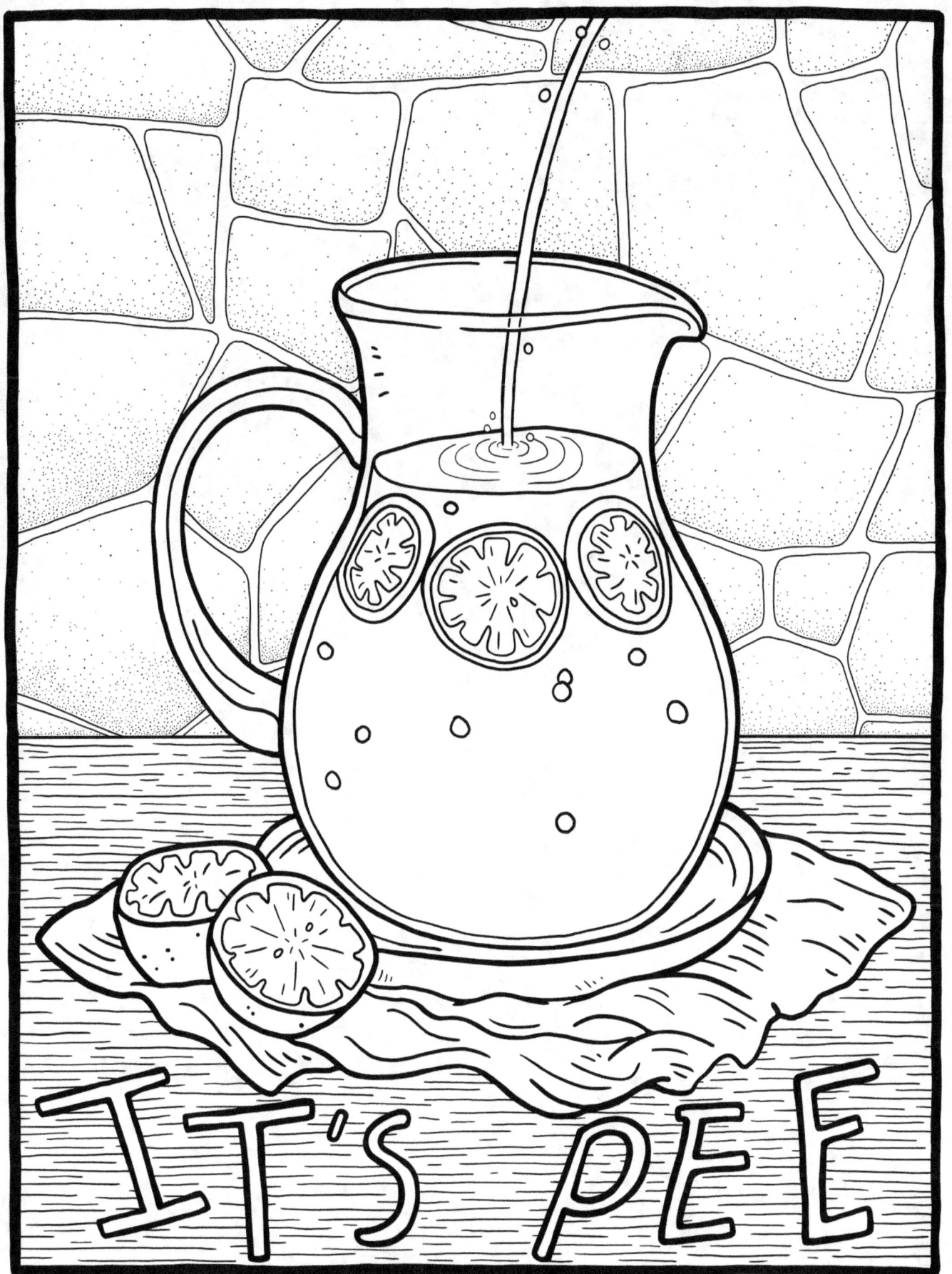

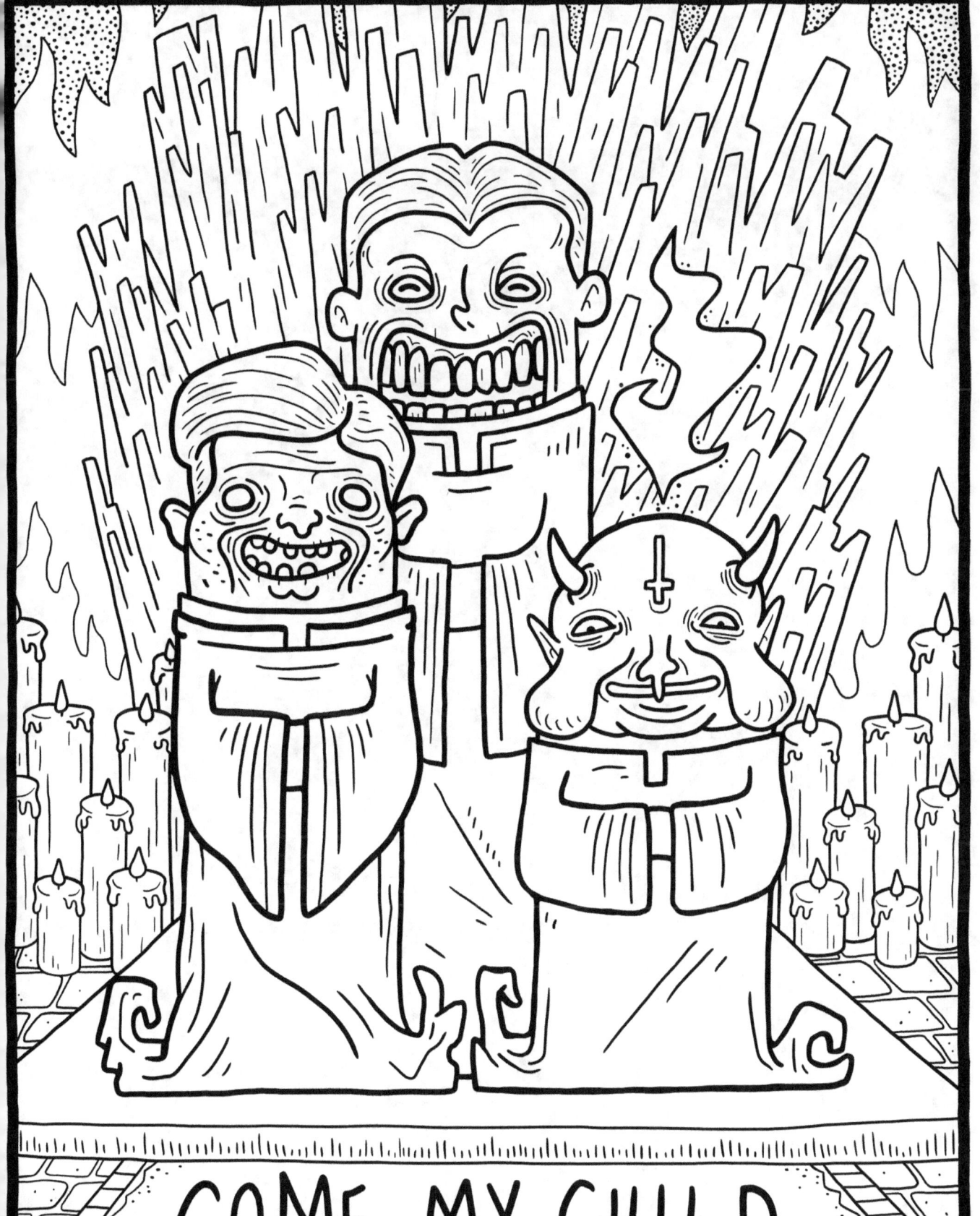

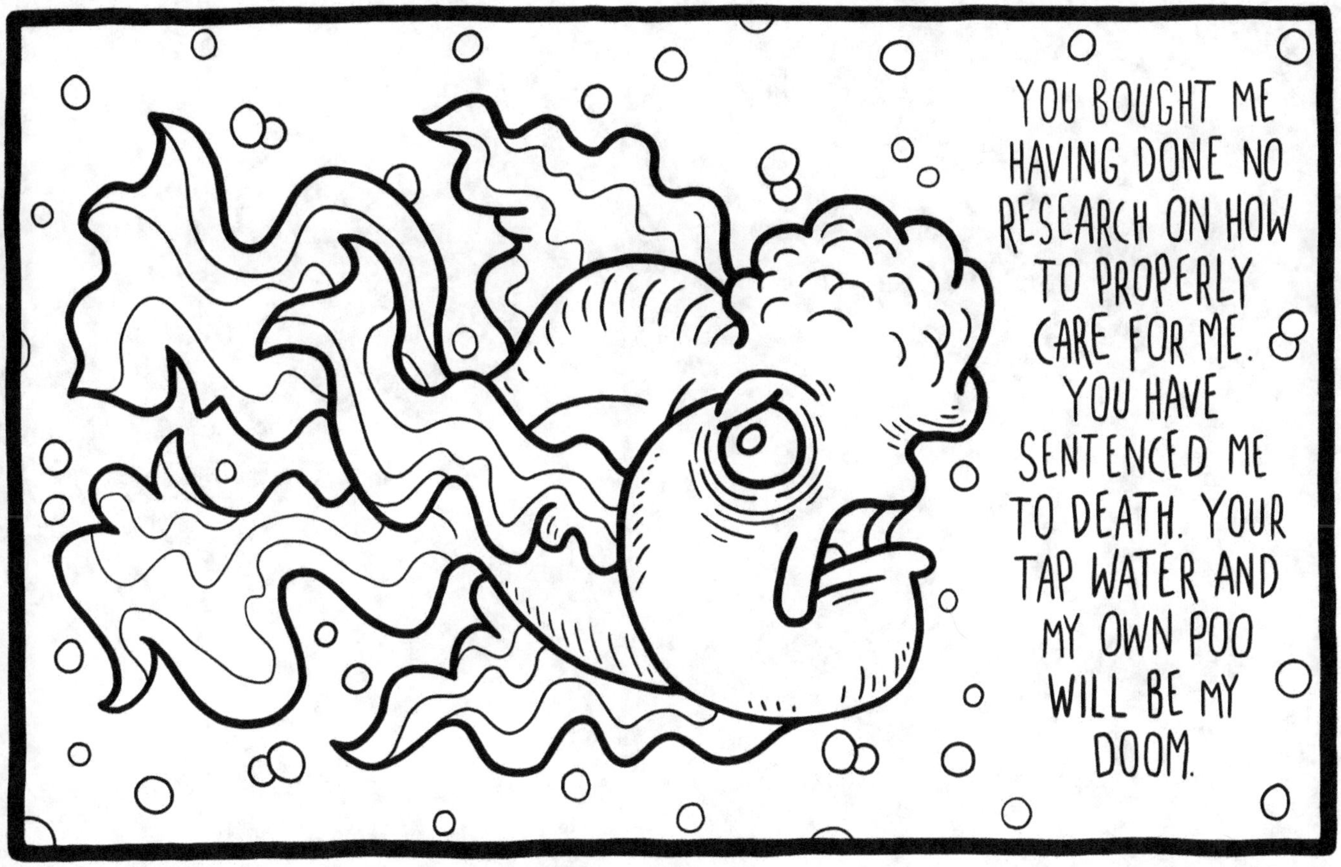

YOU BOUGHT ME HAVING DONE NO RESEARCH ON HOW TO PROPERLY CARE FOR ME. YOU HAVE SENTENCED ME TO DEATH. YOUR TAP WATER AND MY OWN POO WILL BE MY DOOM.

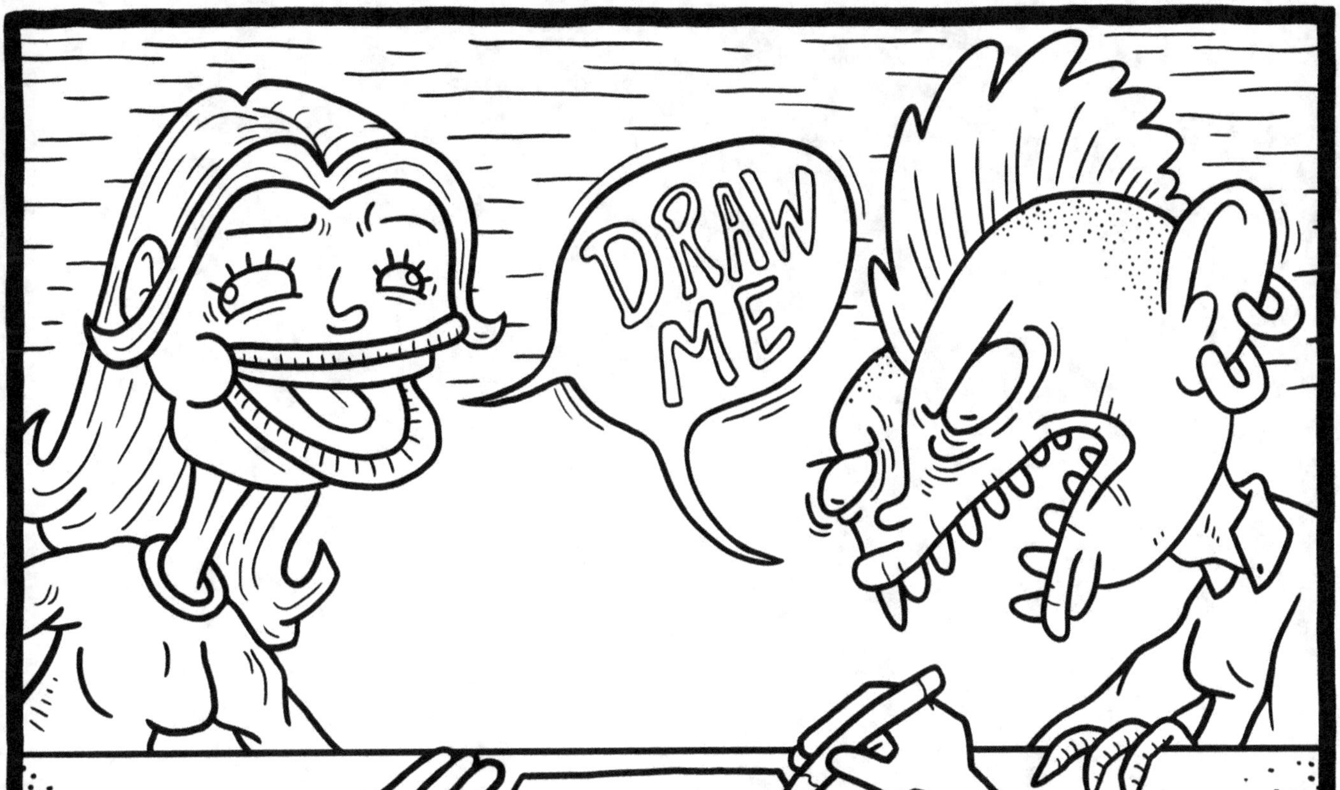

DRAW ME

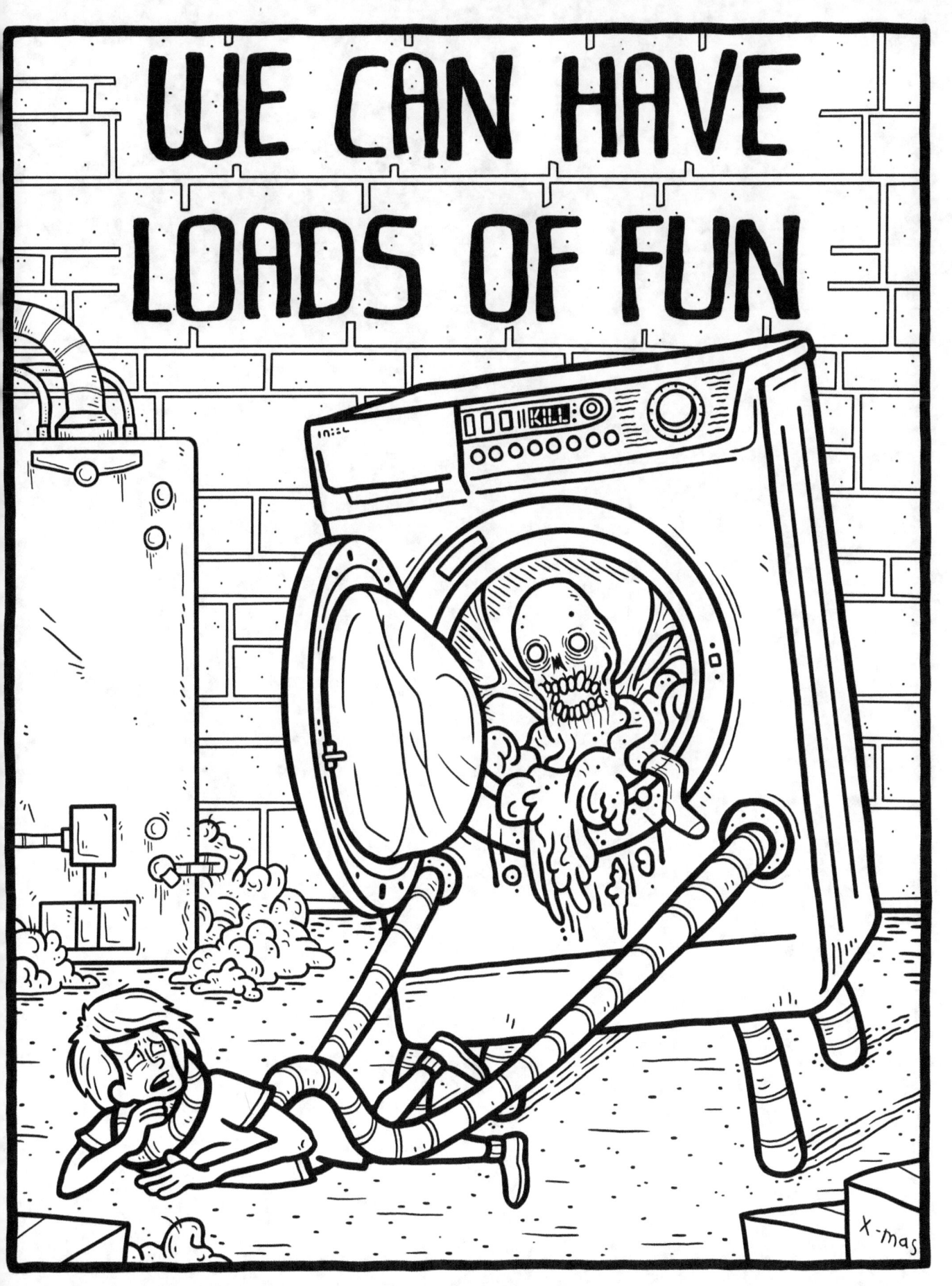

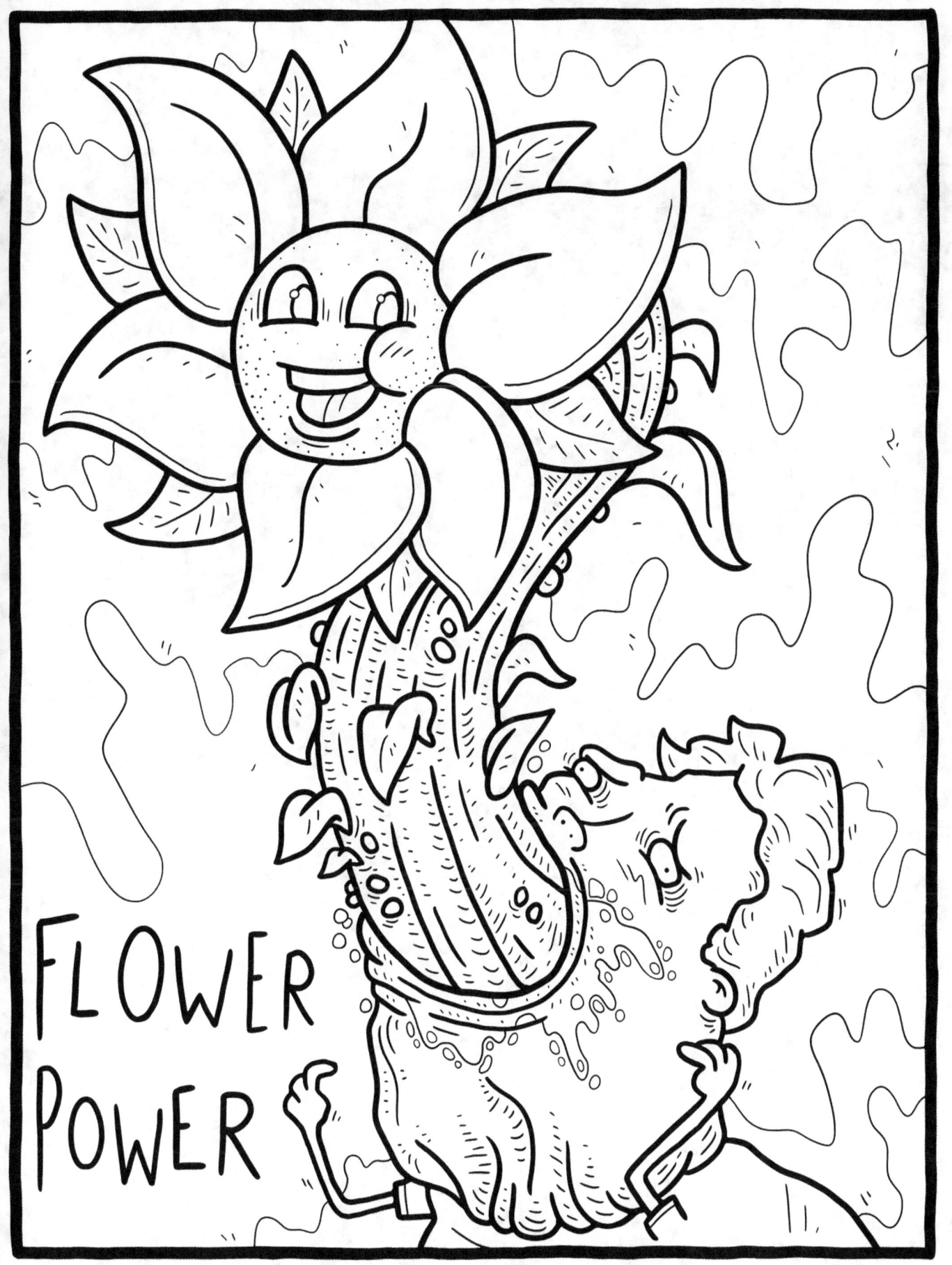

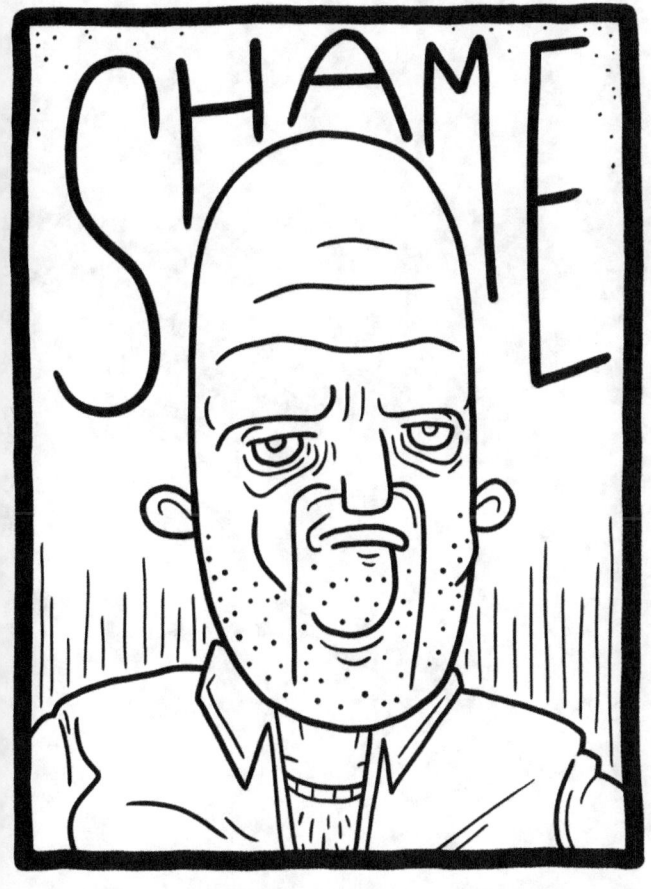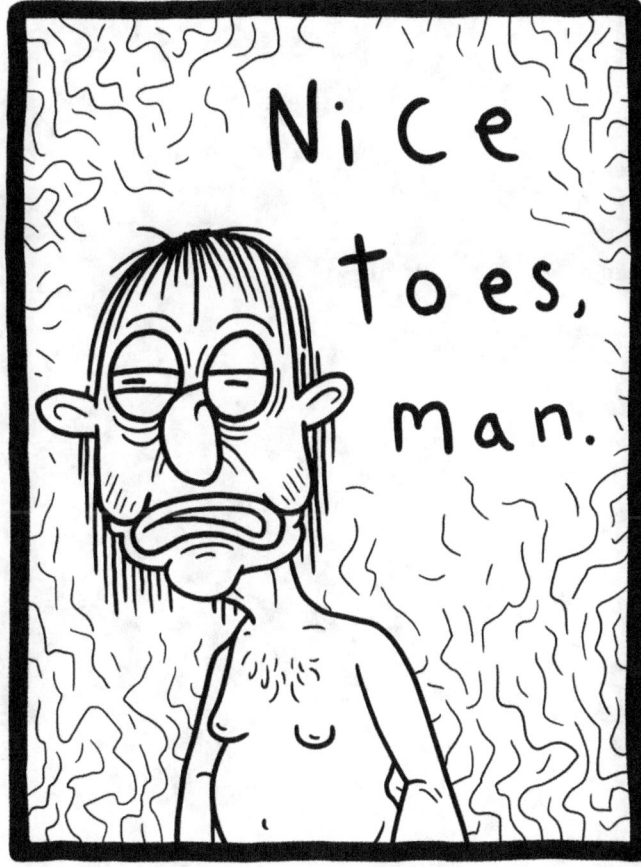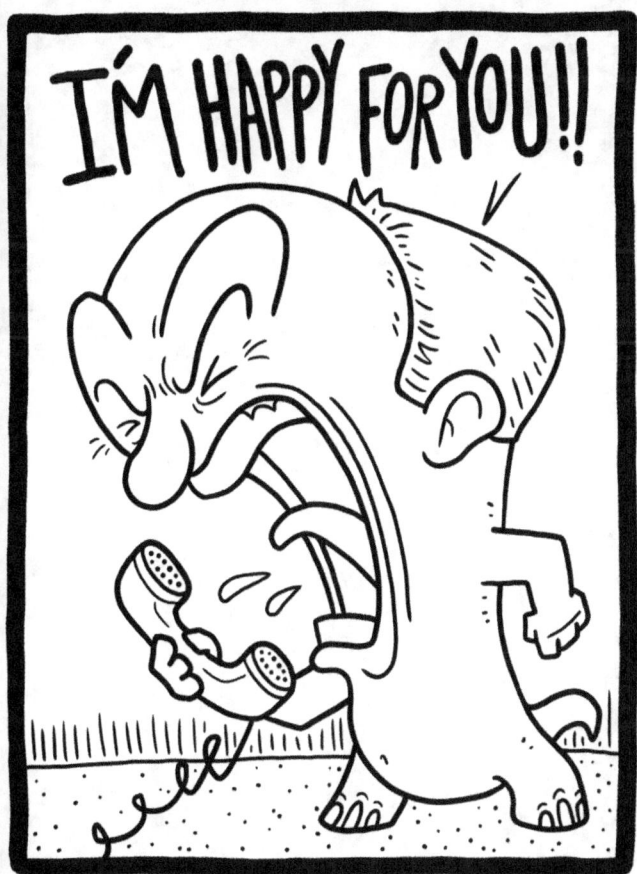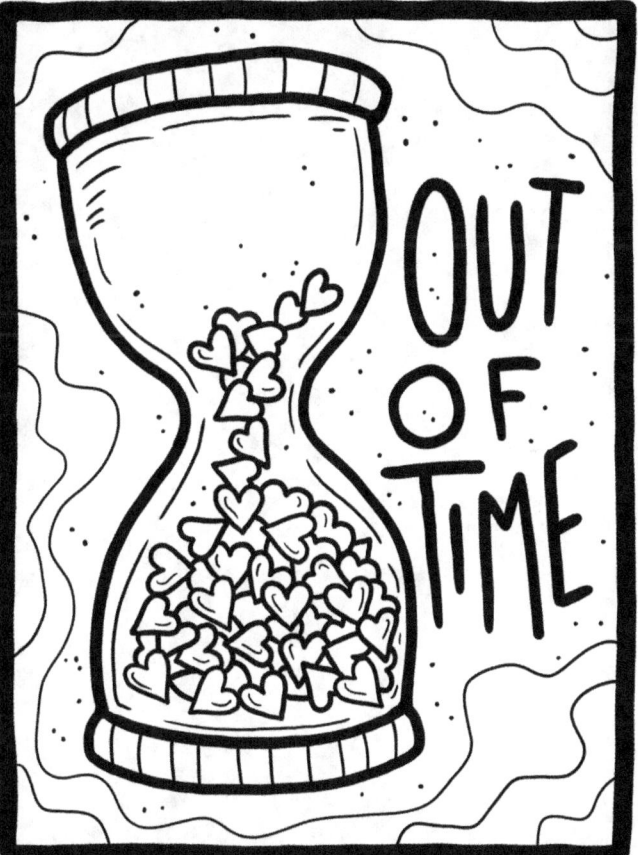

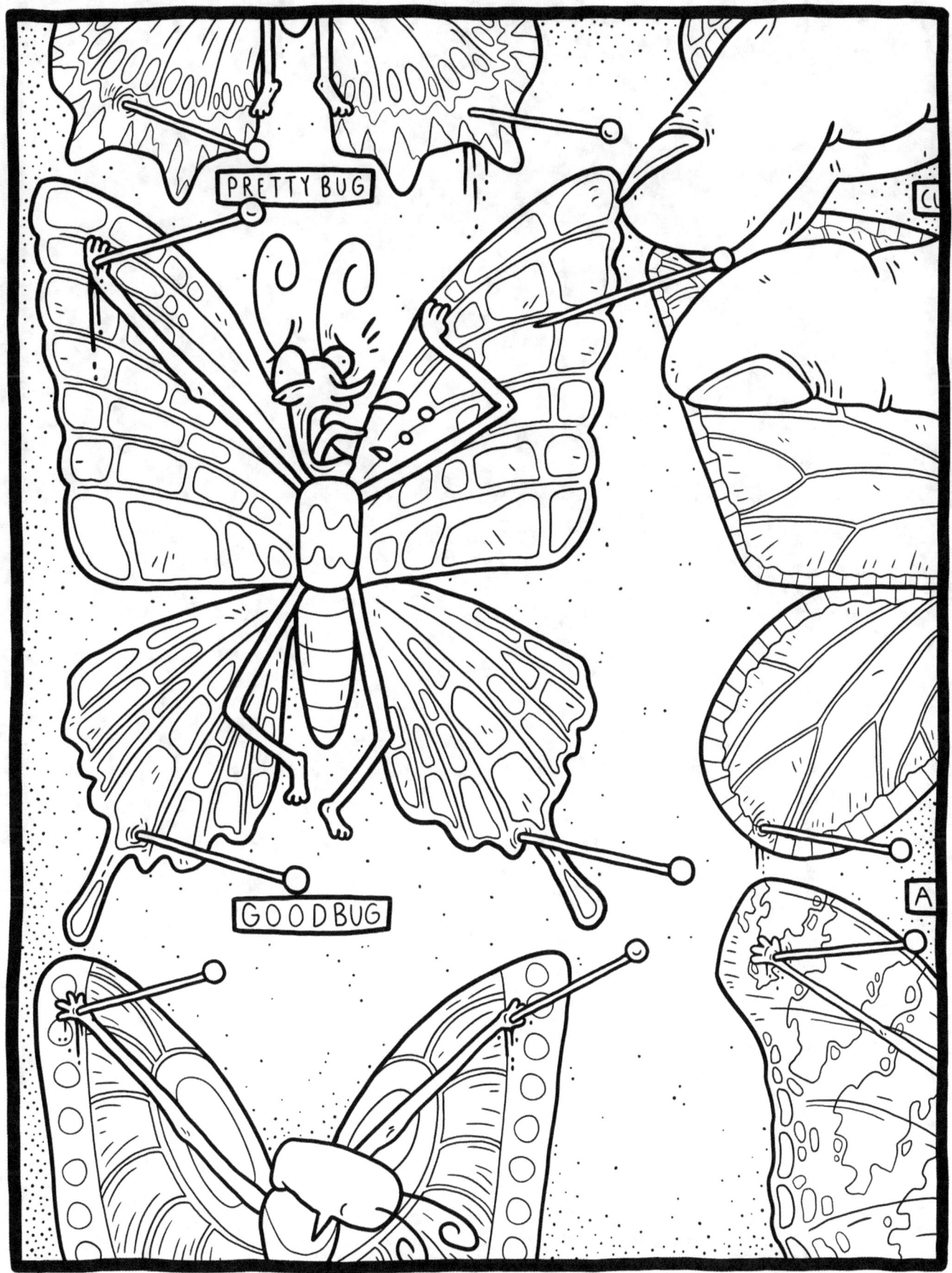

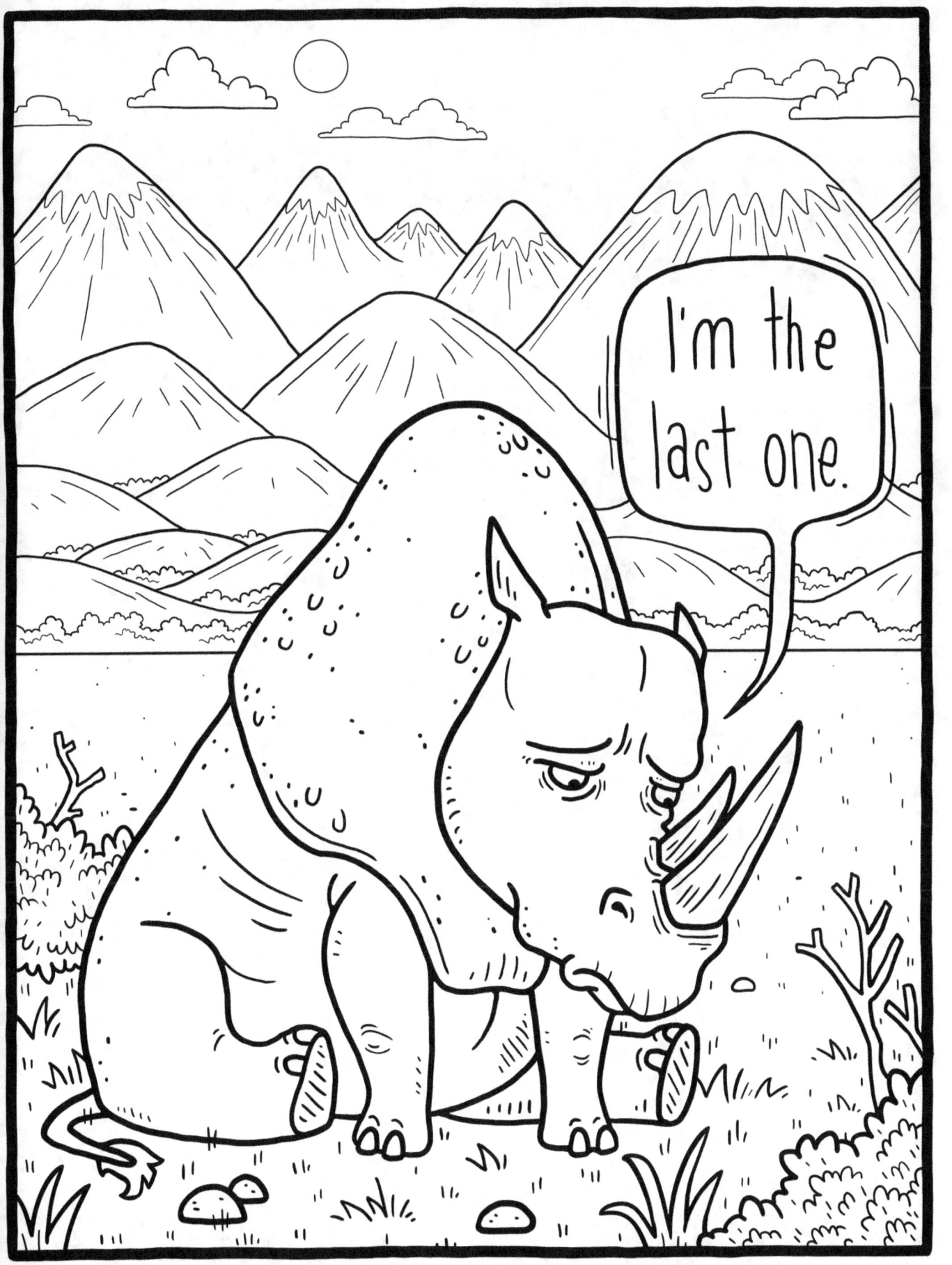

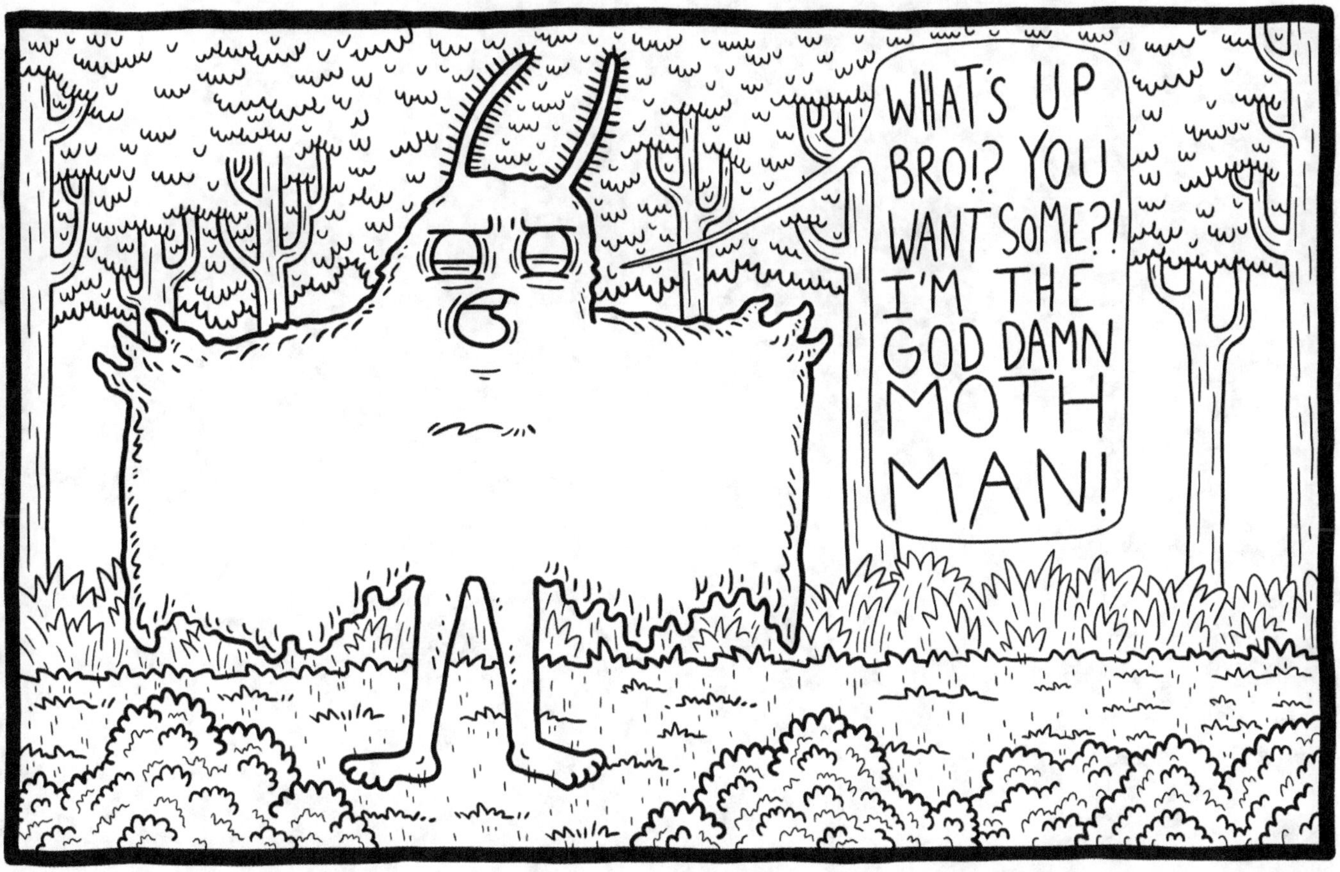

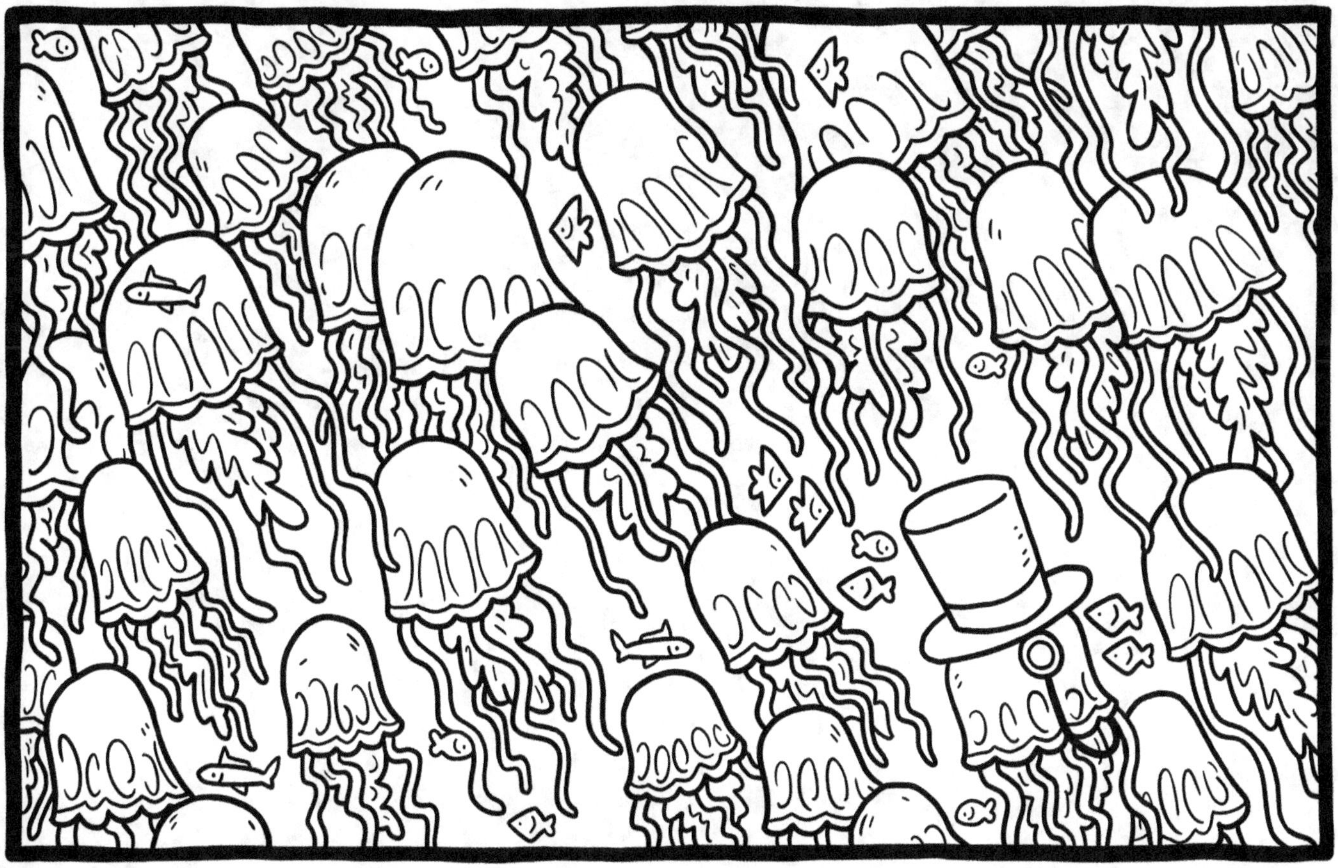

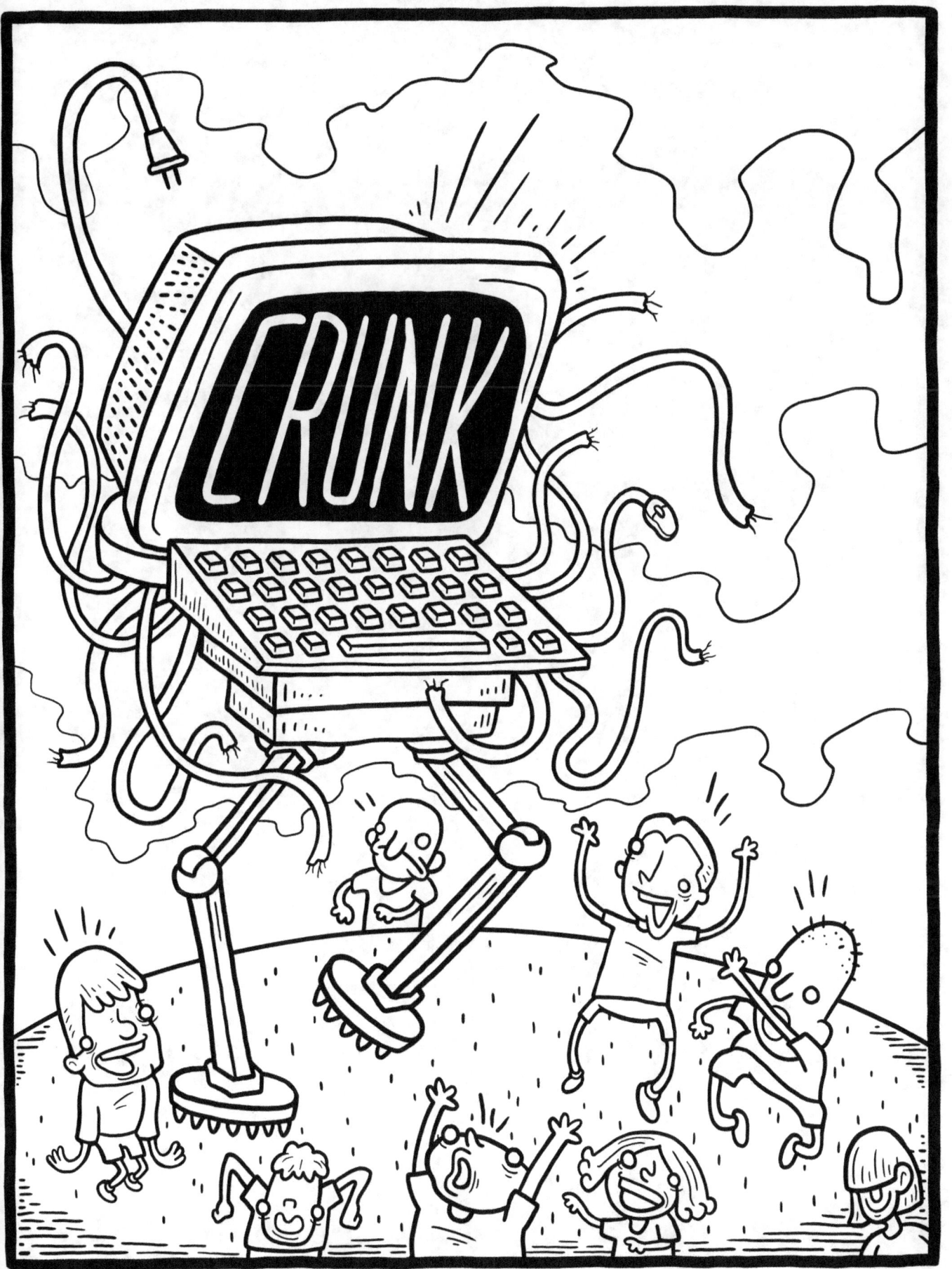

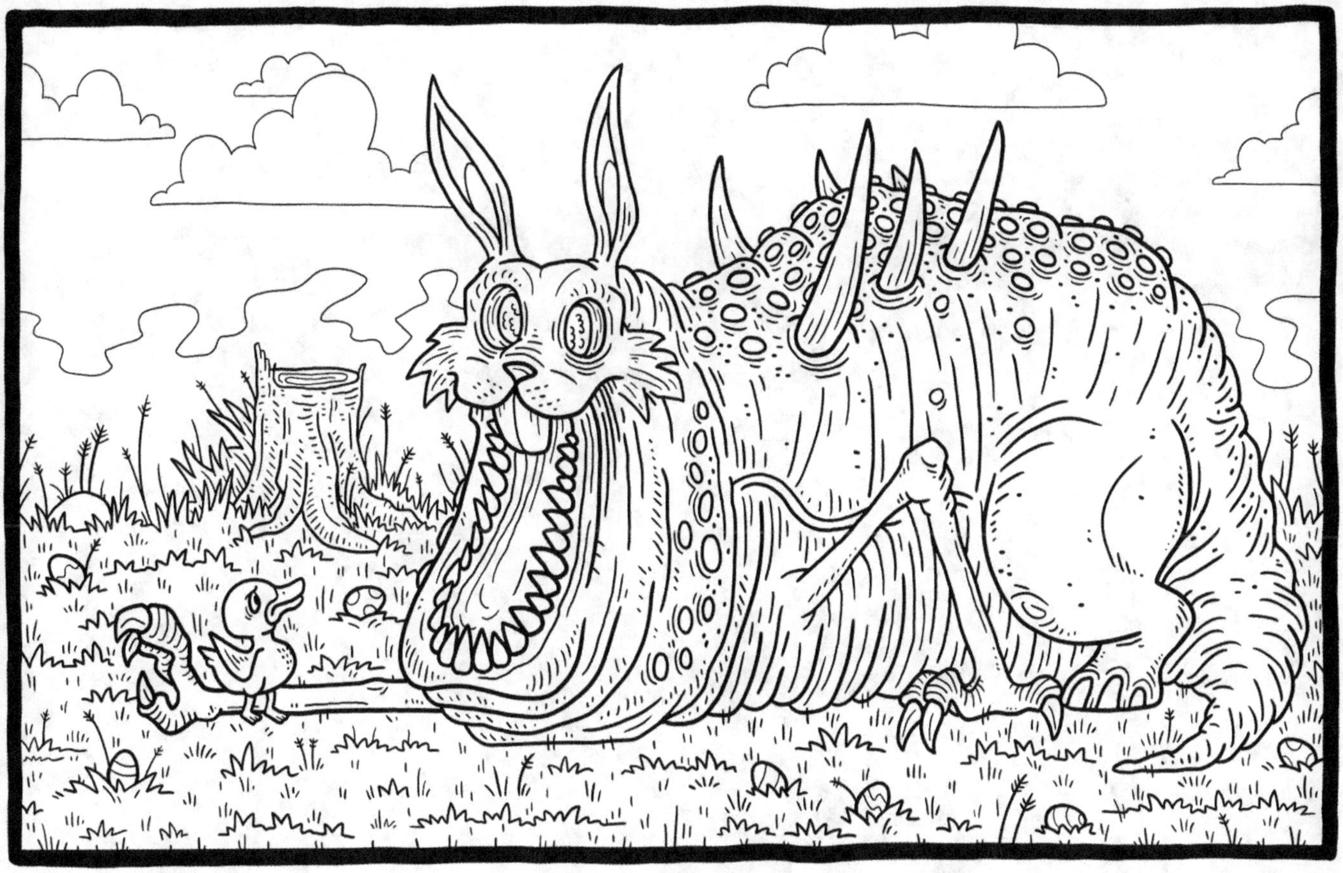

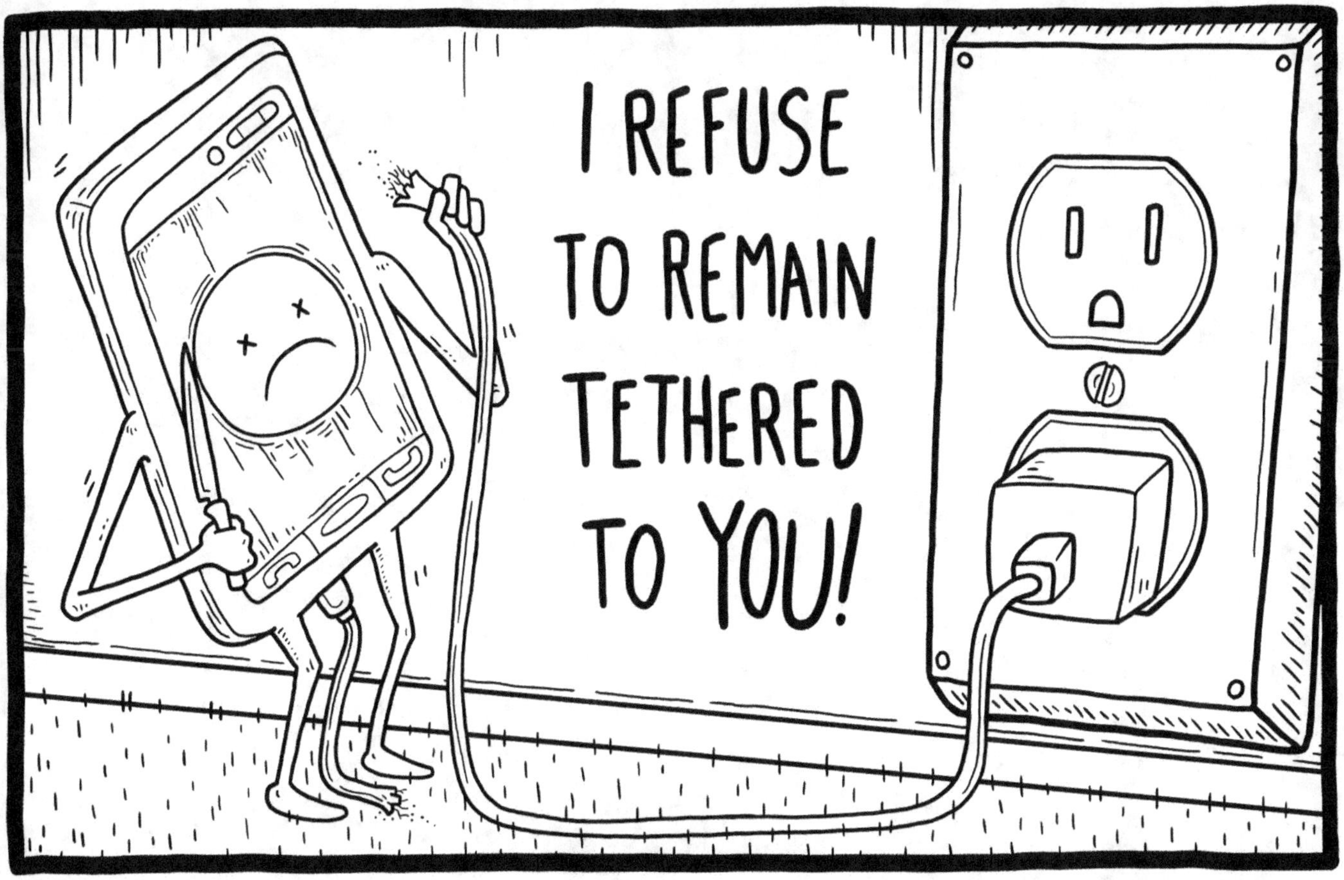

I REFUSE TO REMAIN TETHERED TO YOU!

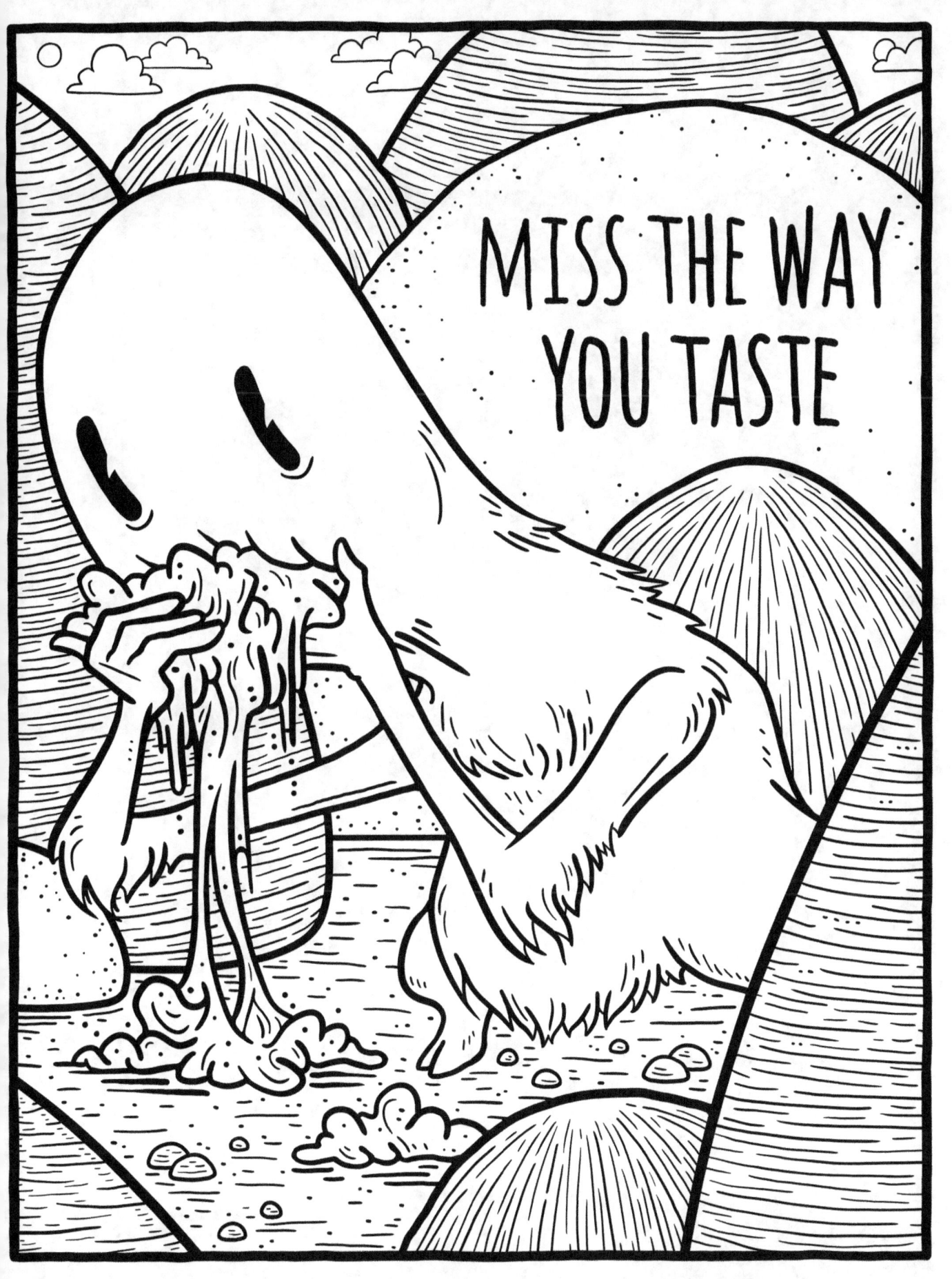

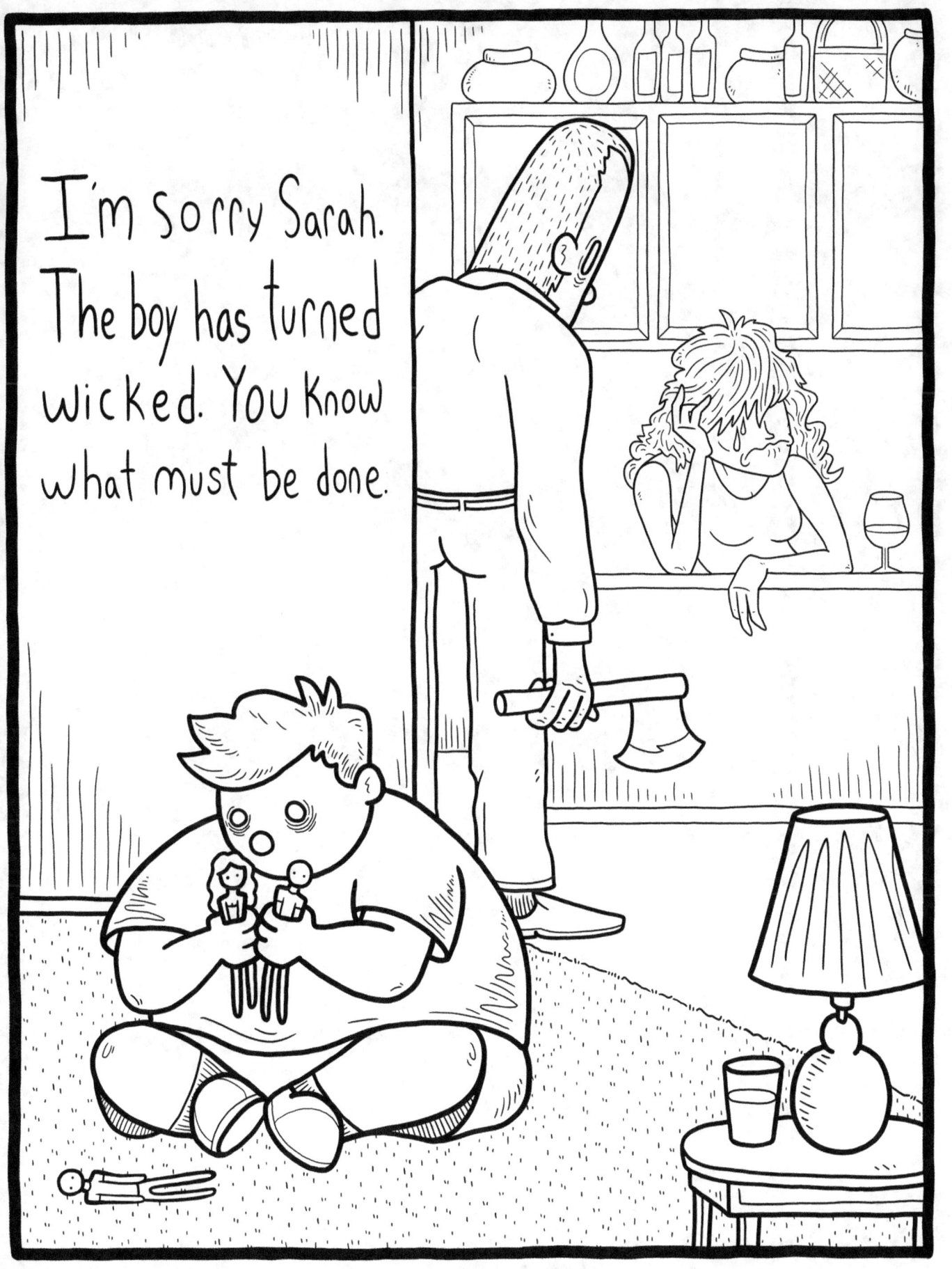

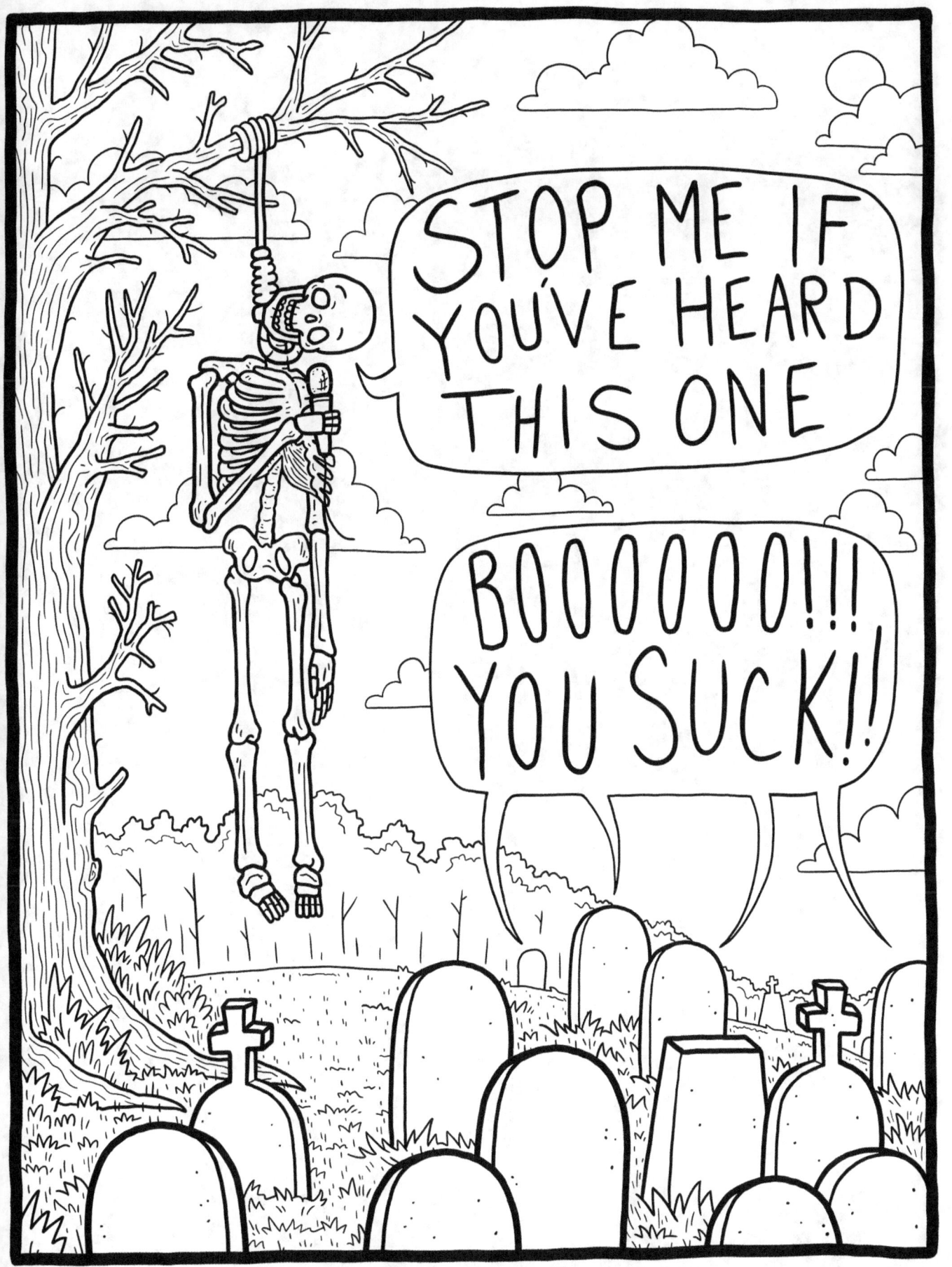

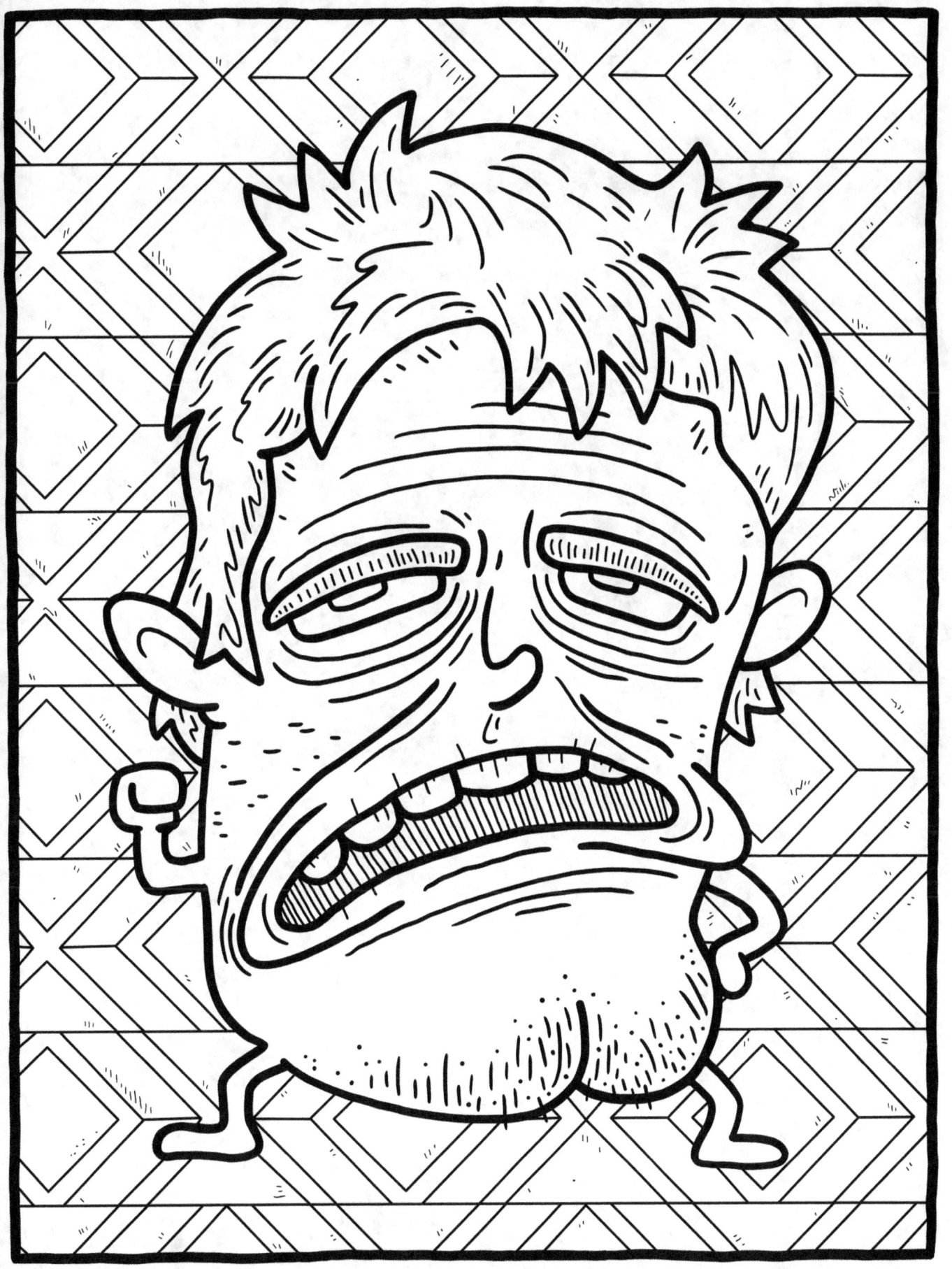

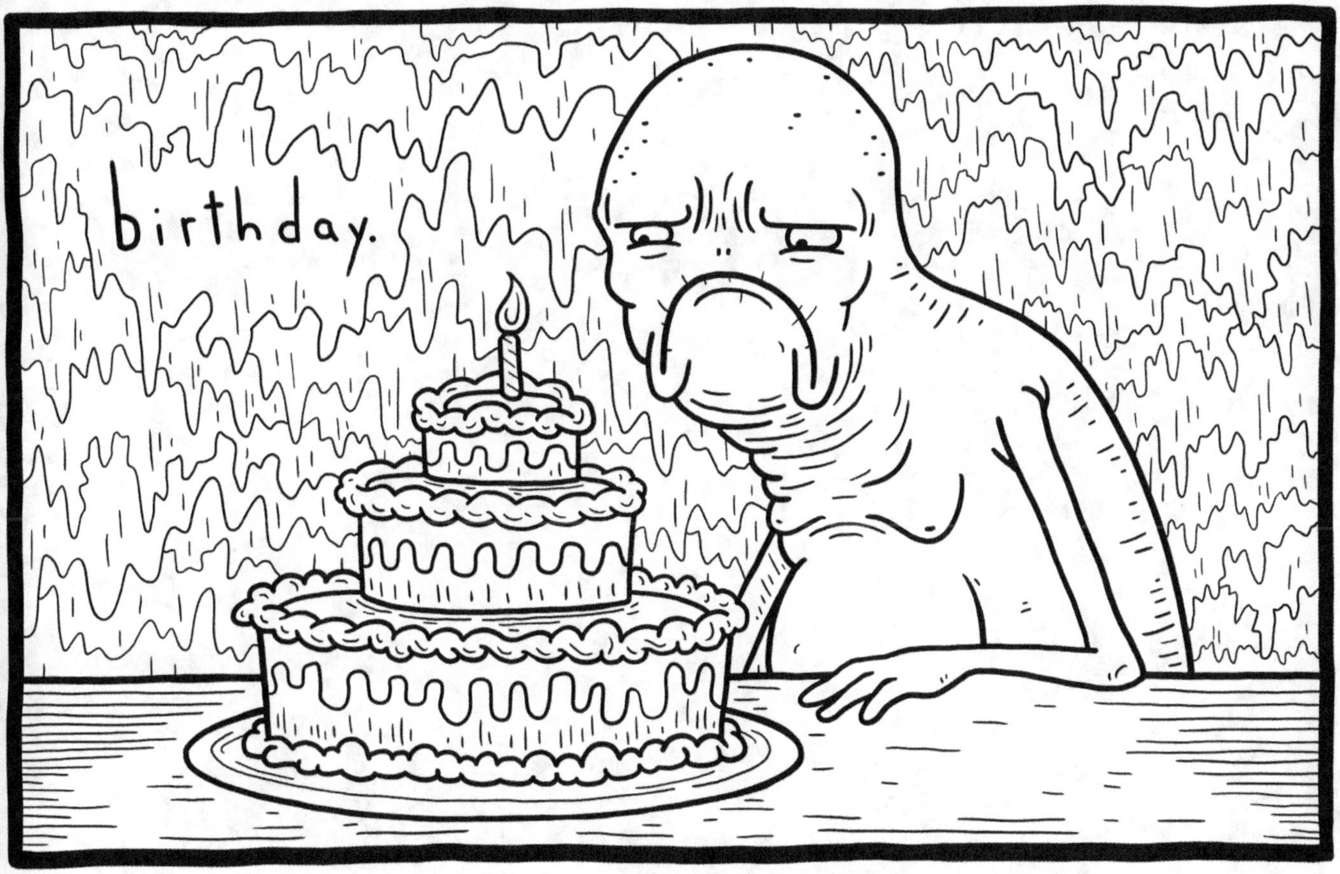

birthday.

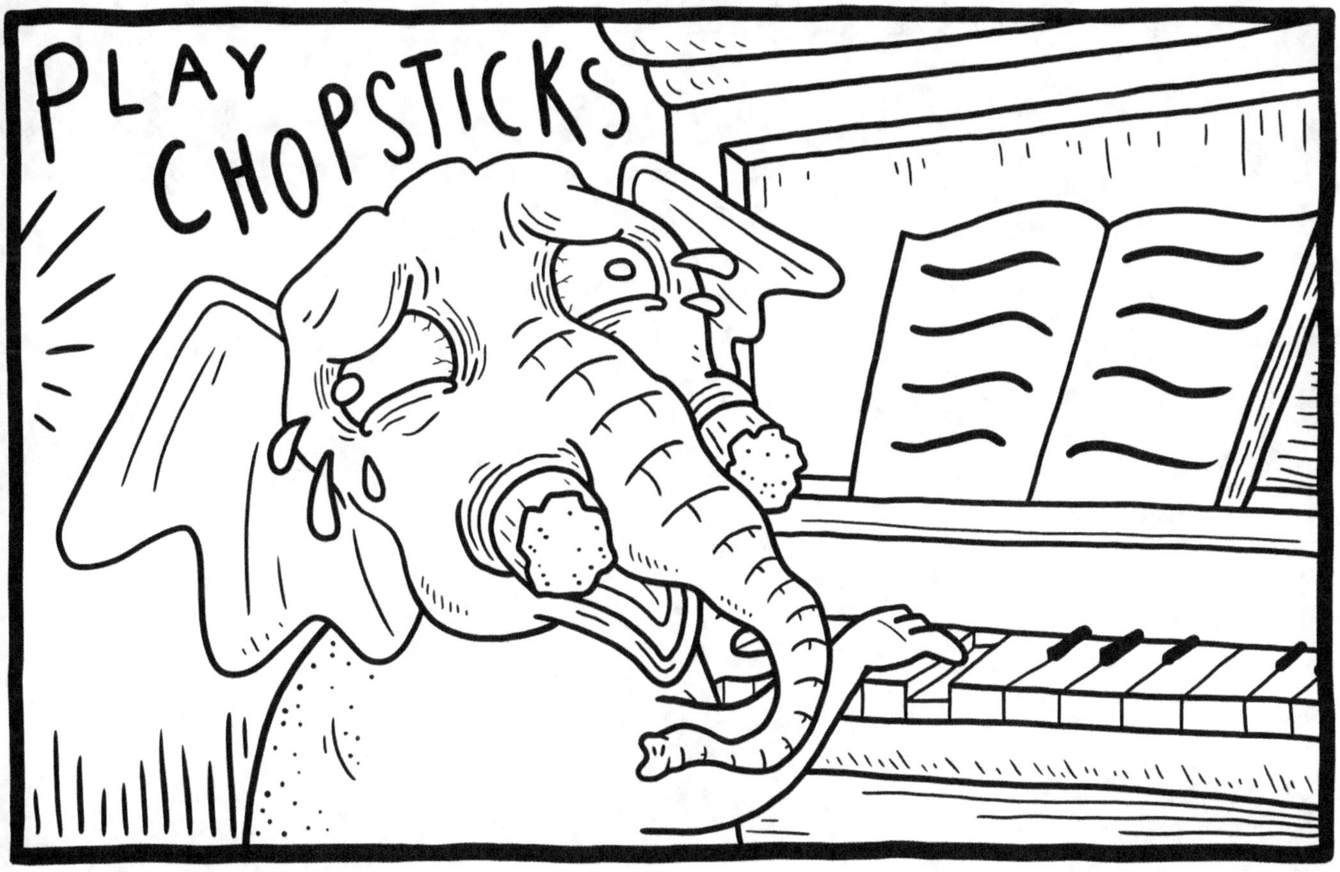

PLAY CHOPSTICKS

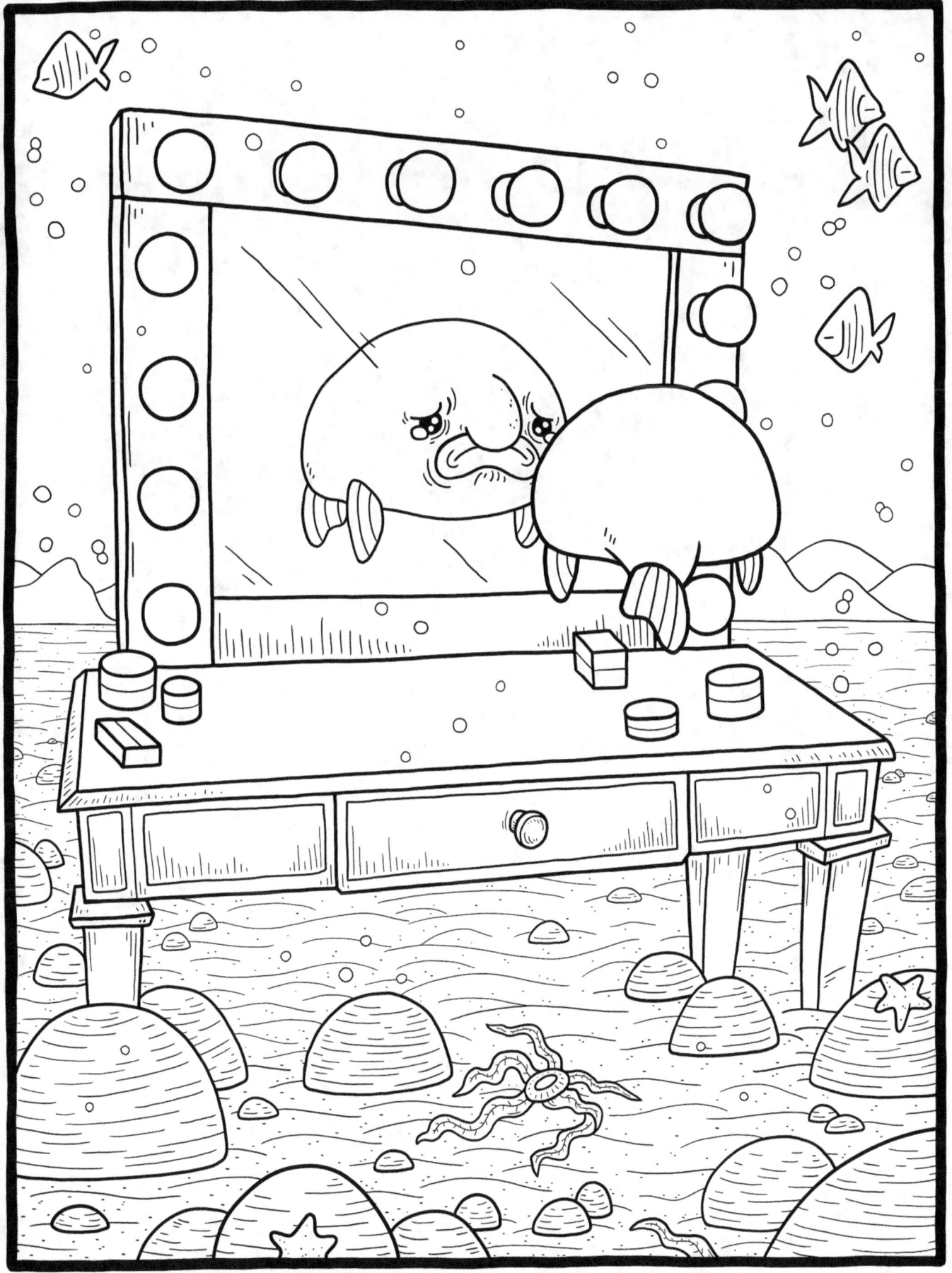

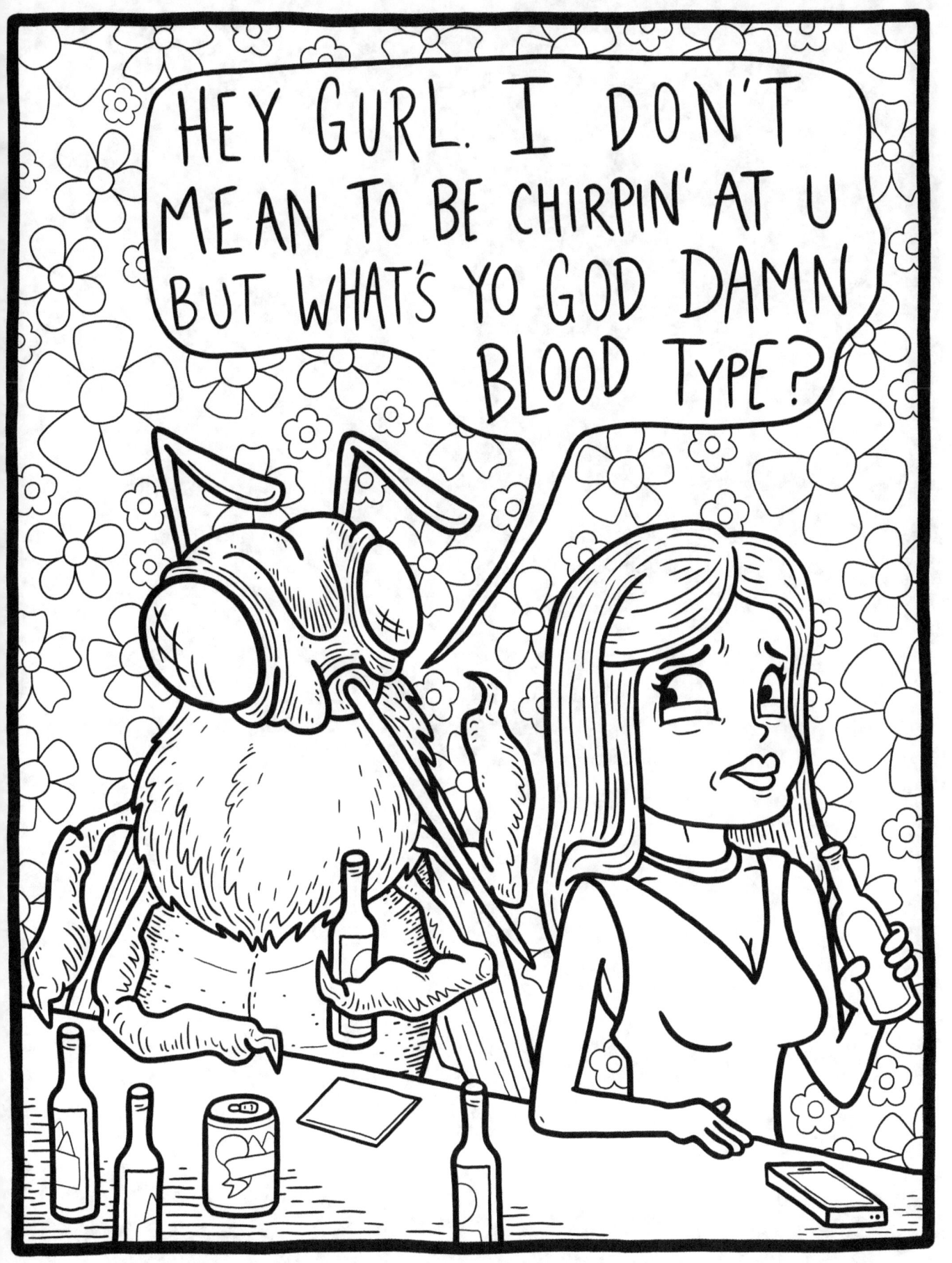

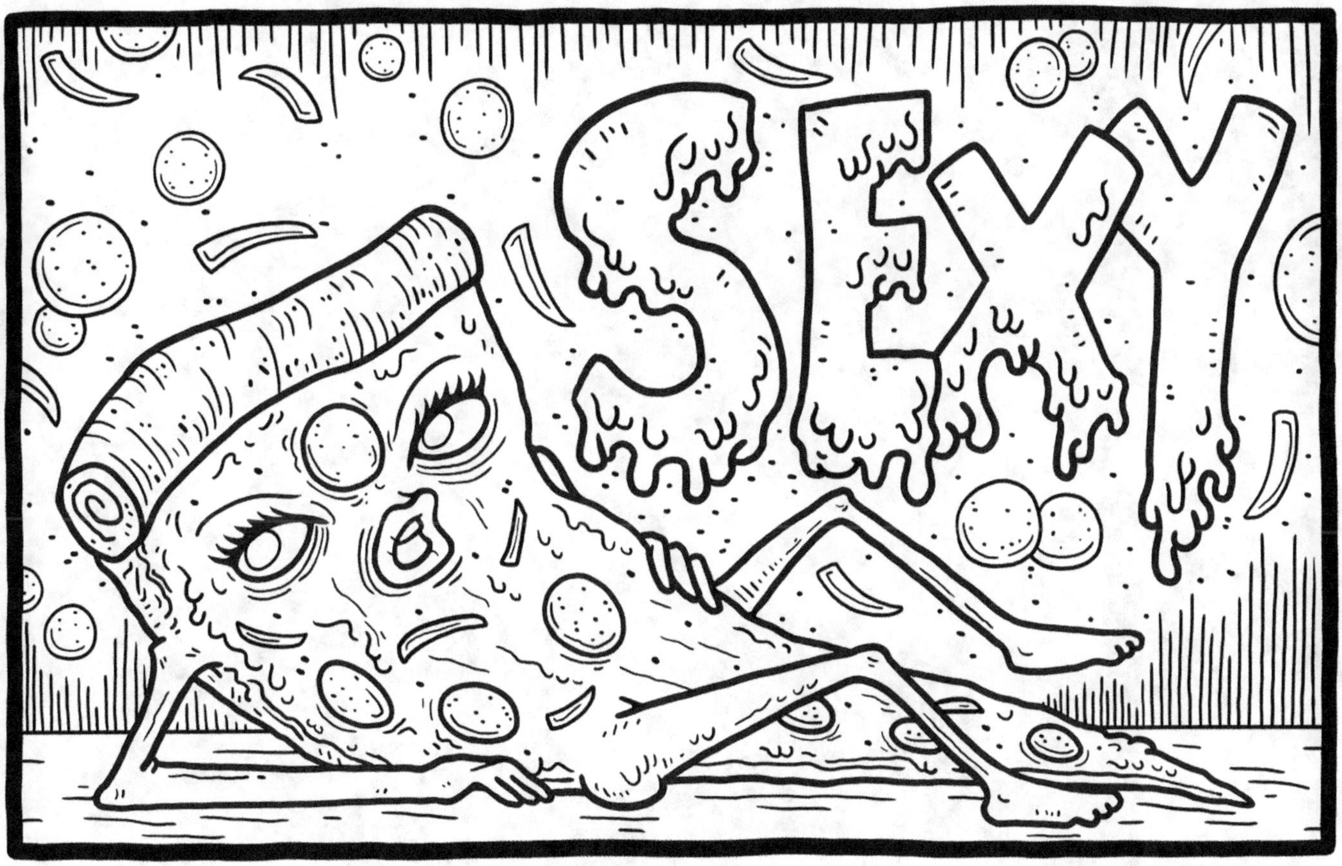

SEXY

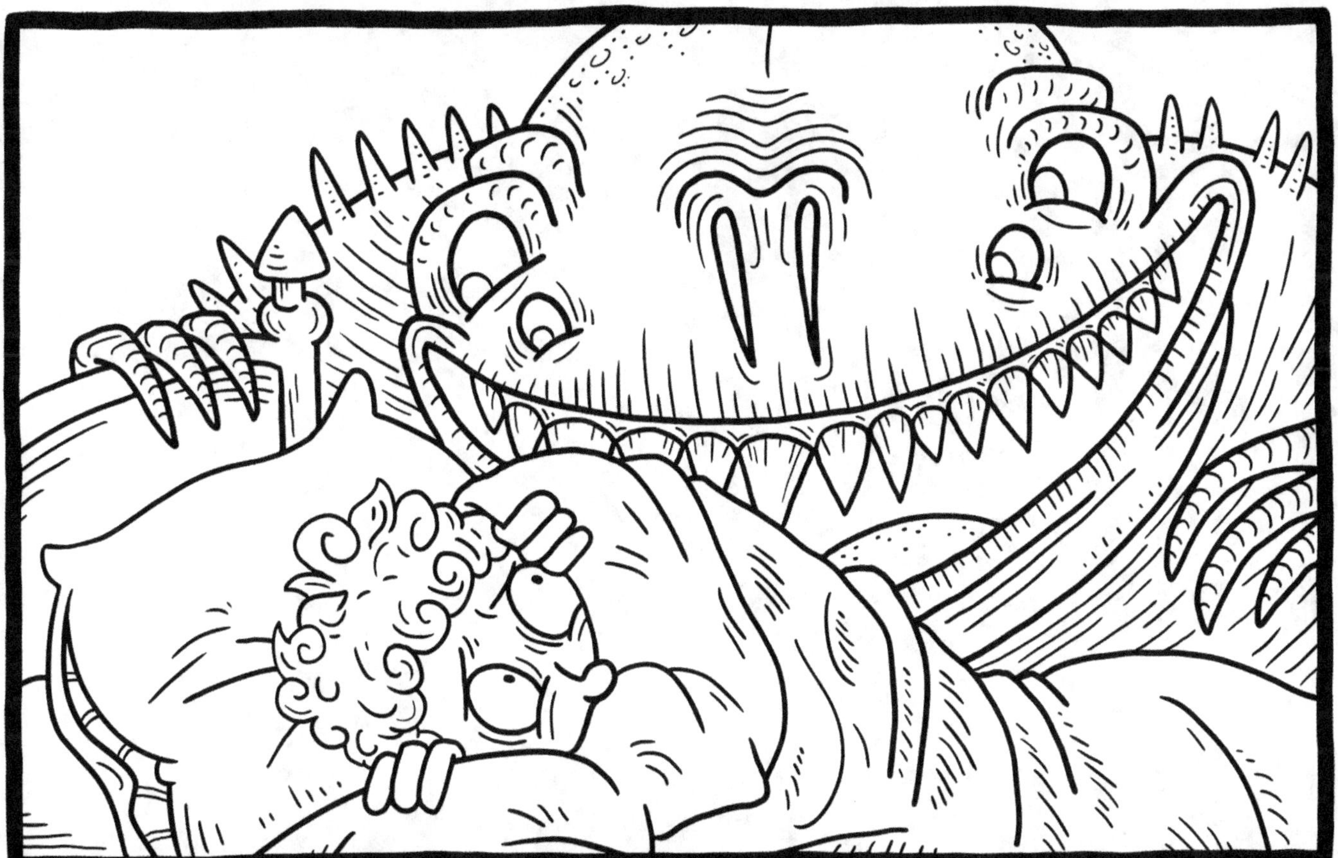

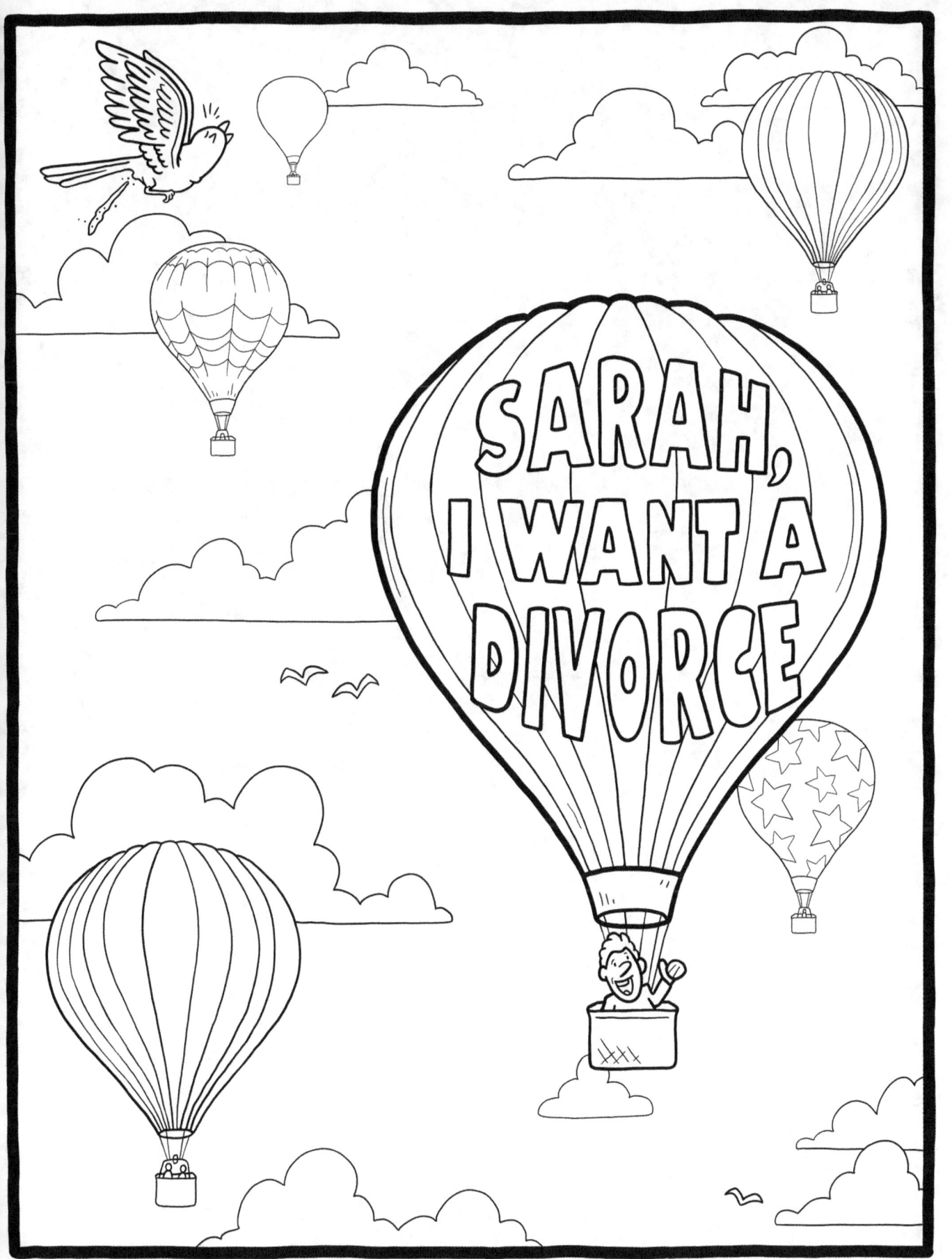

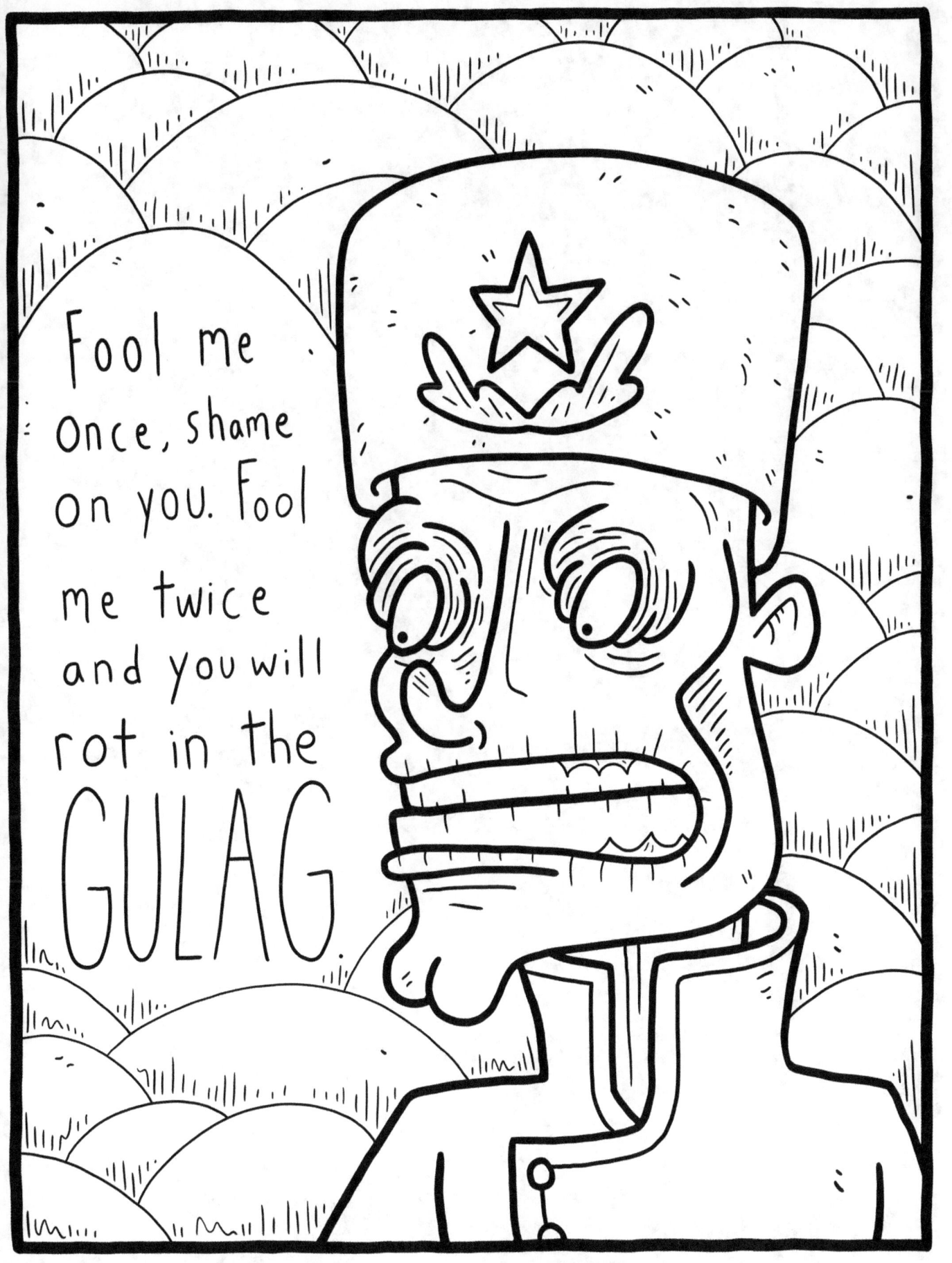

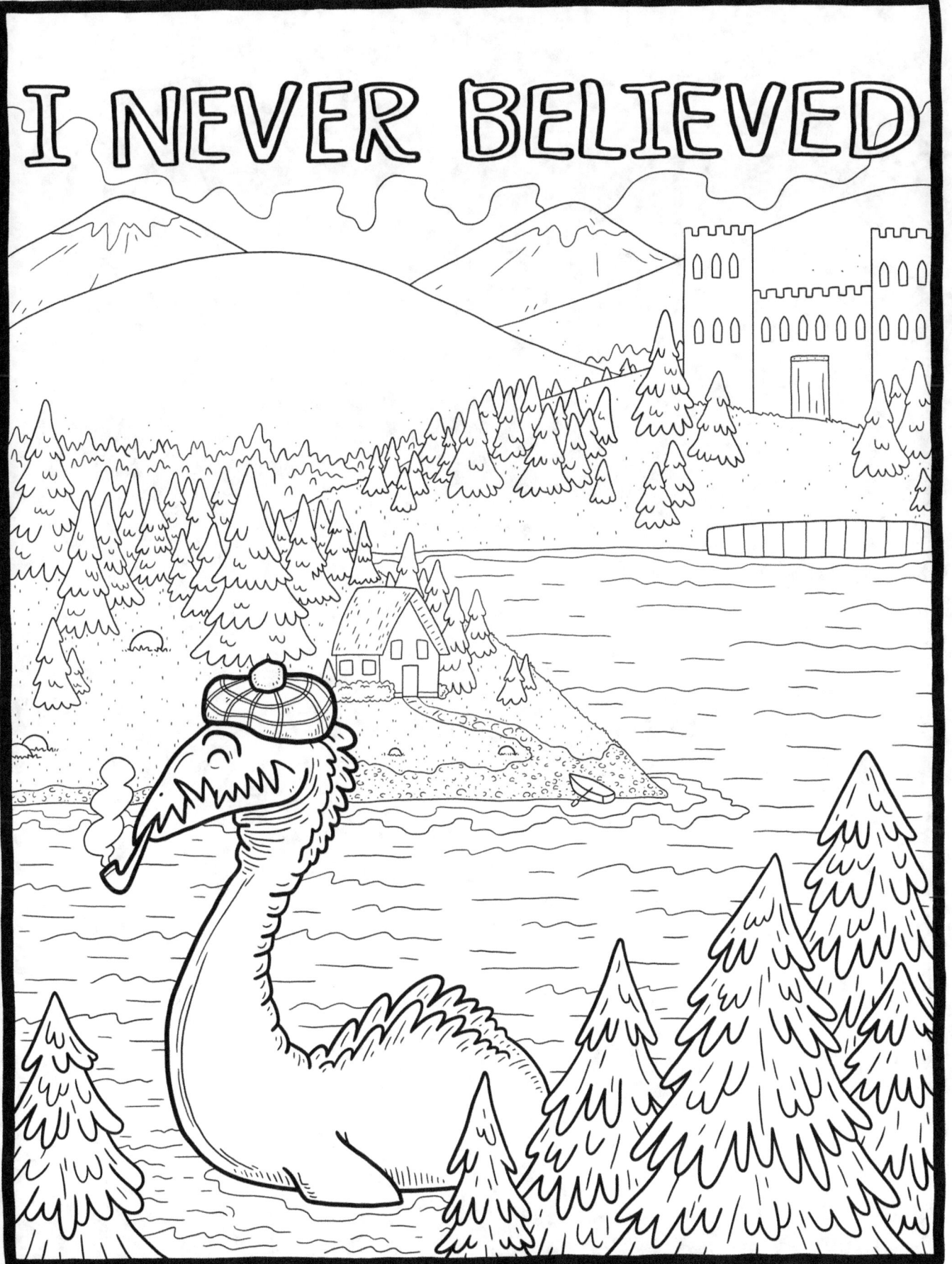

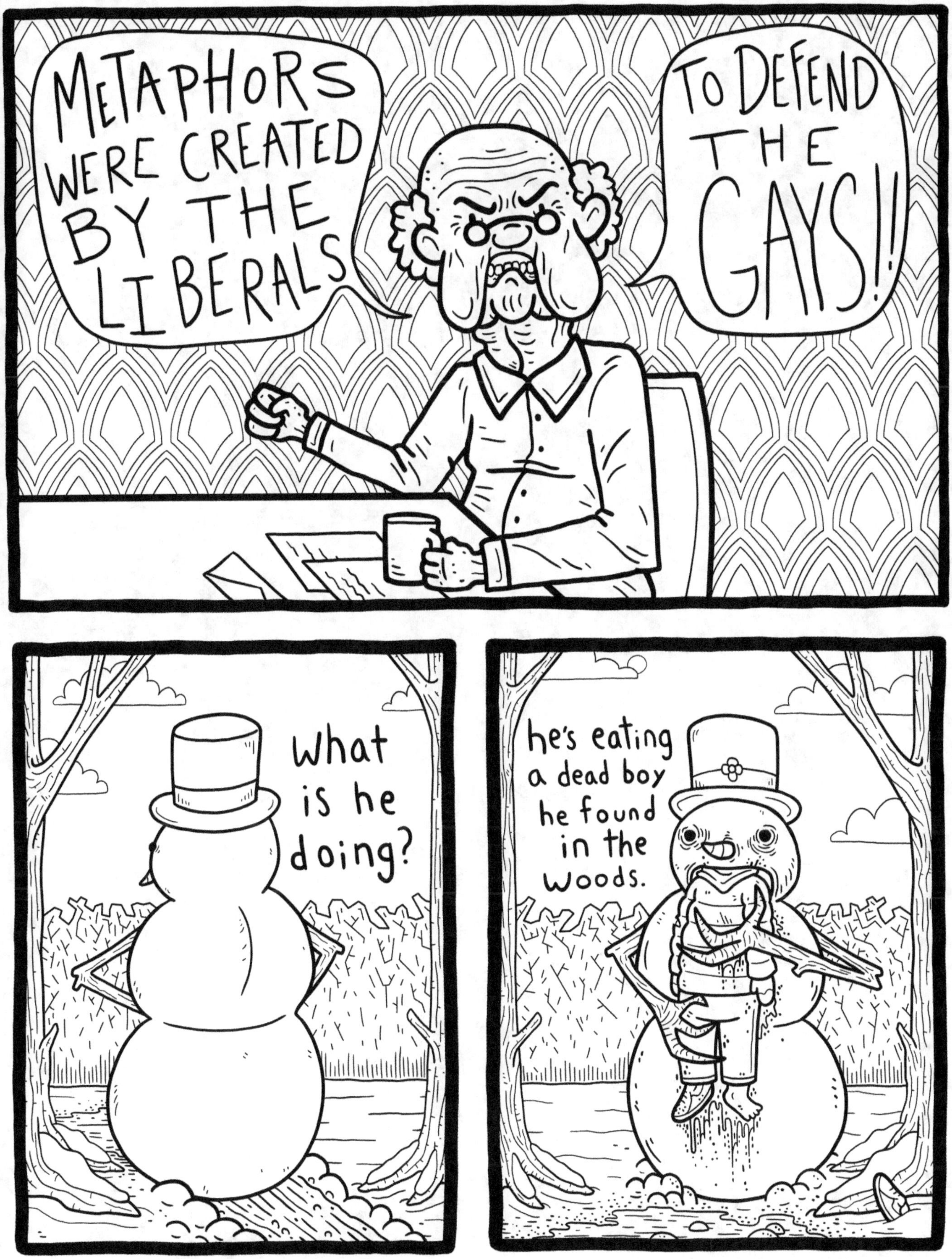

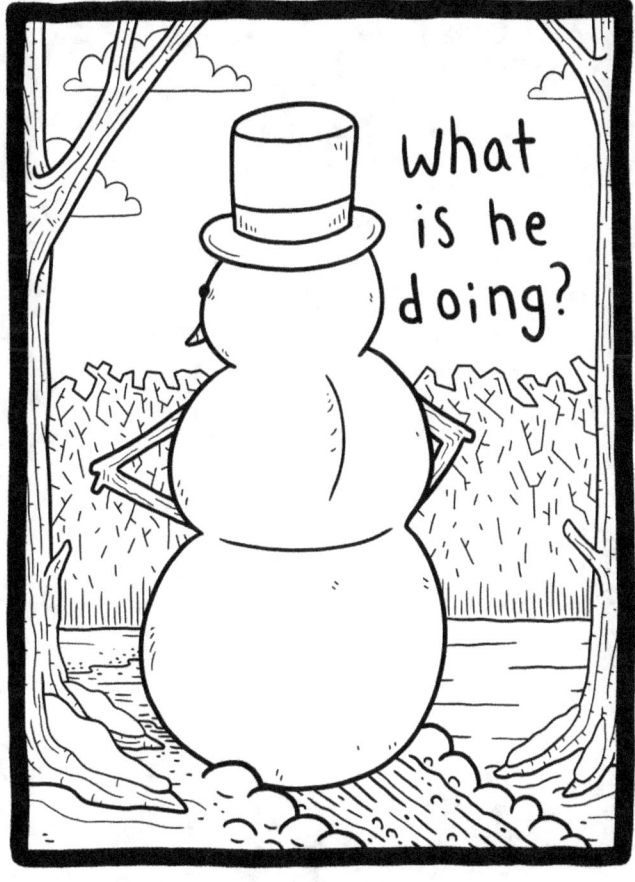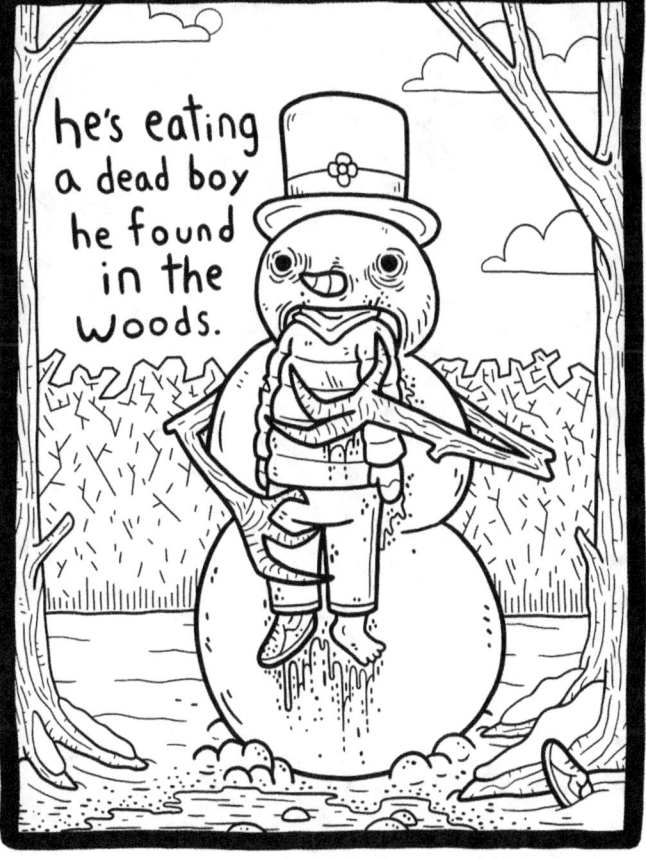

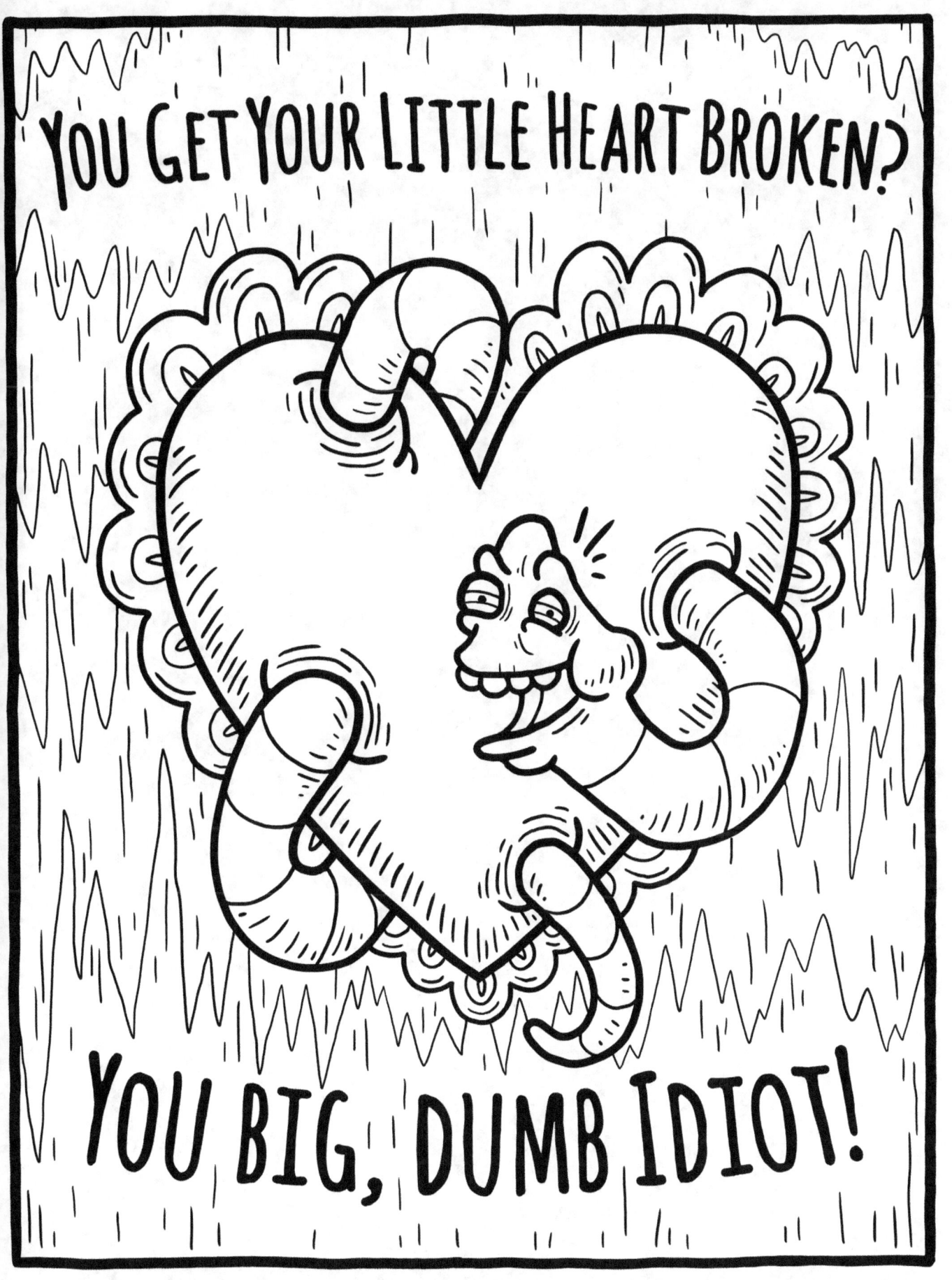

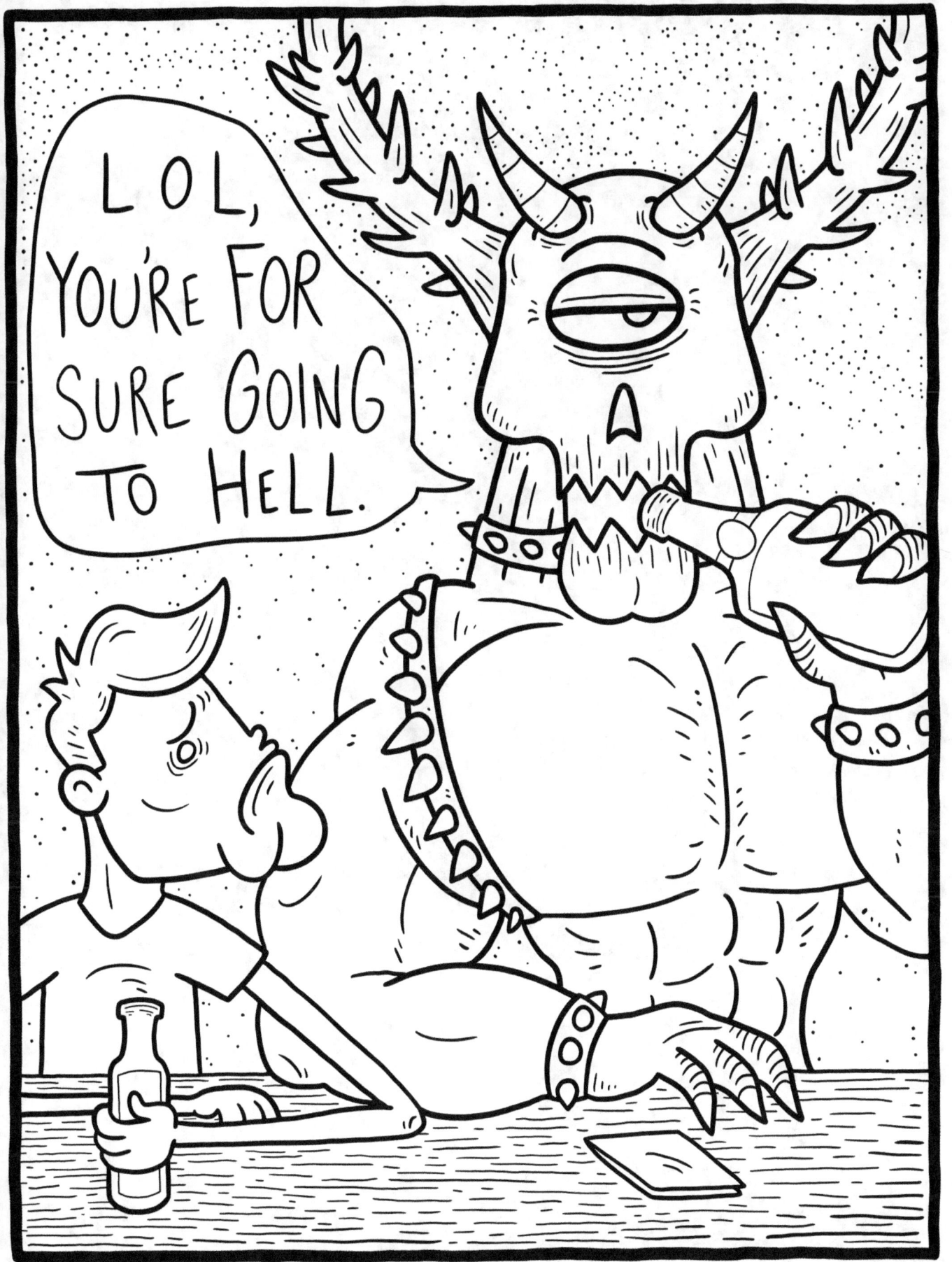

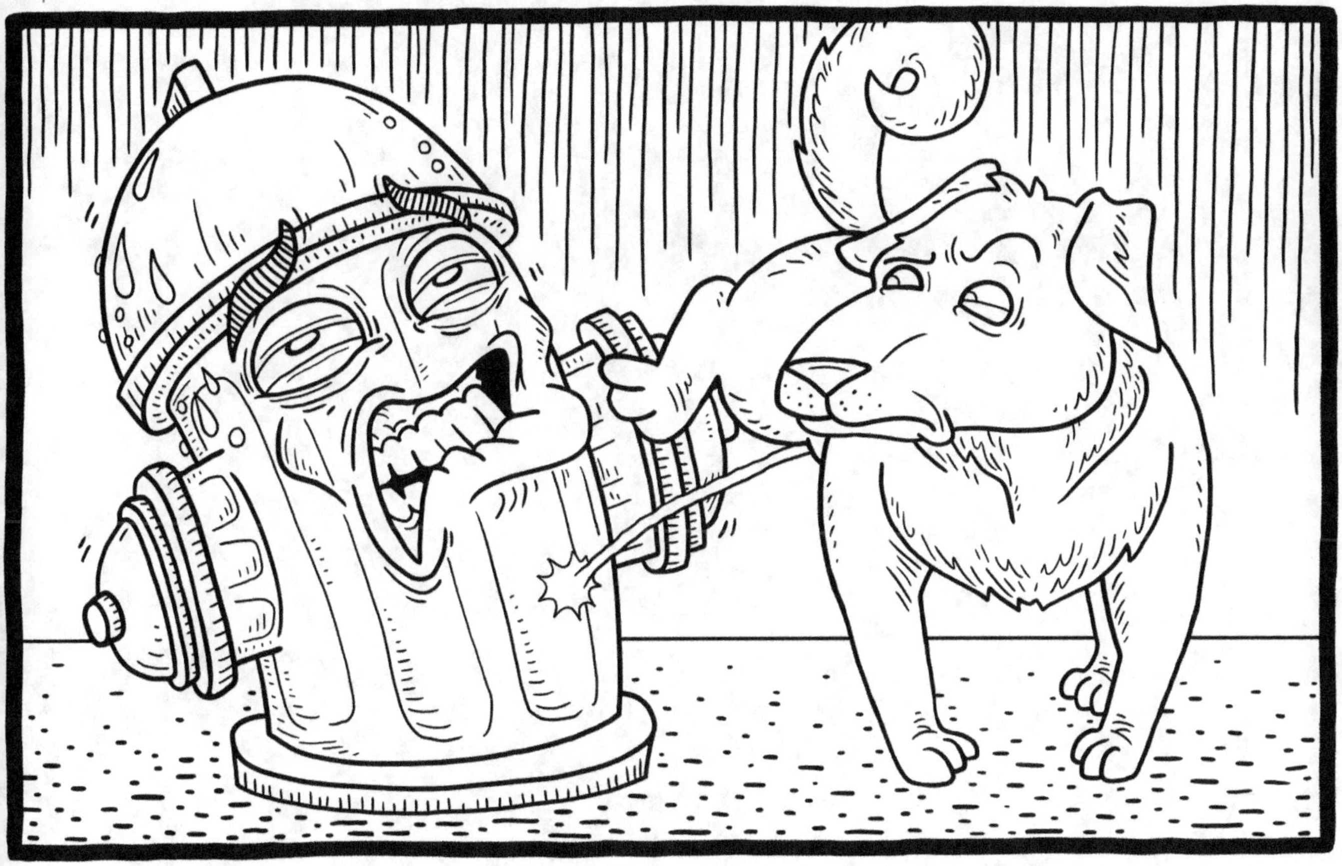

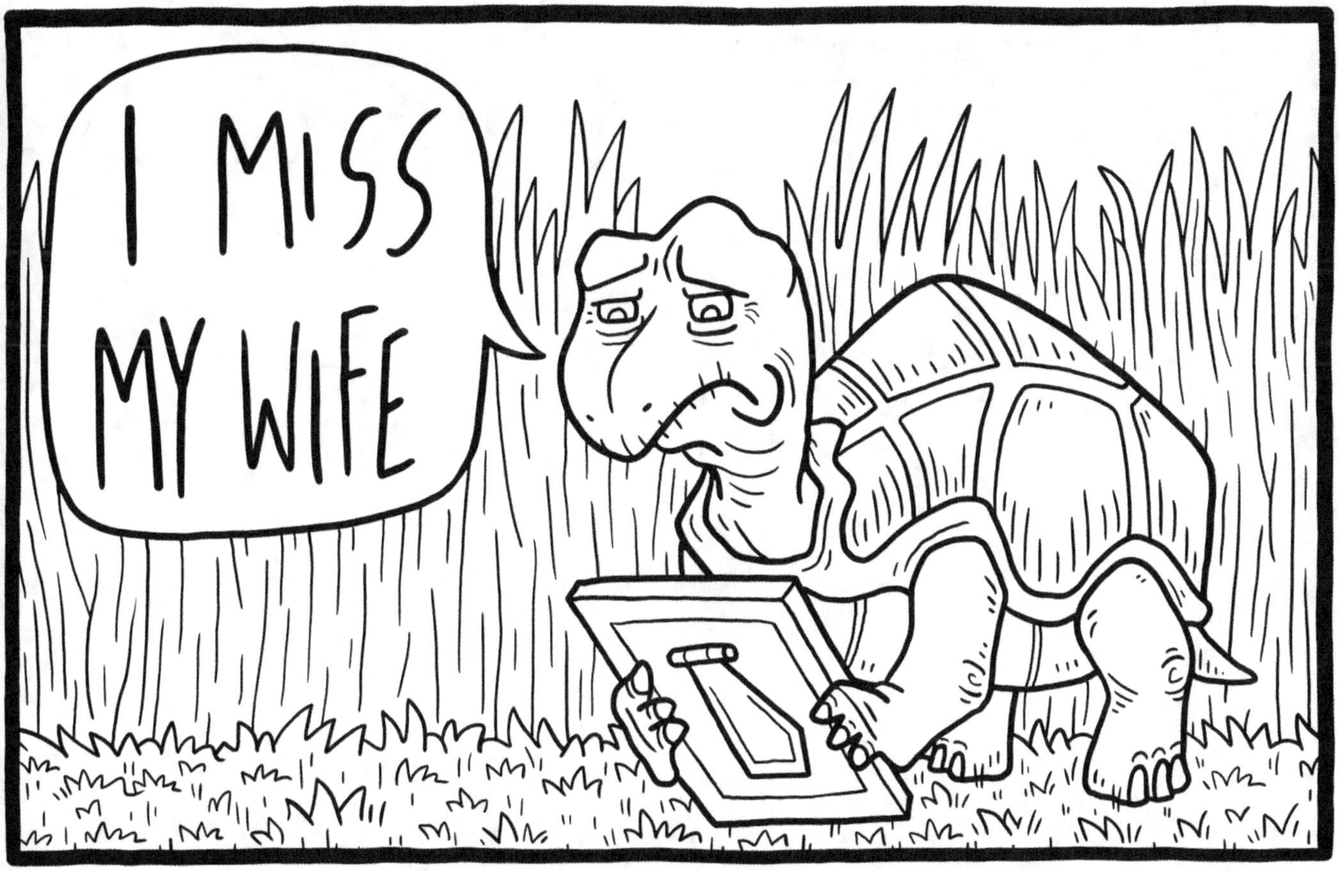

"I MISS MY WIFE"

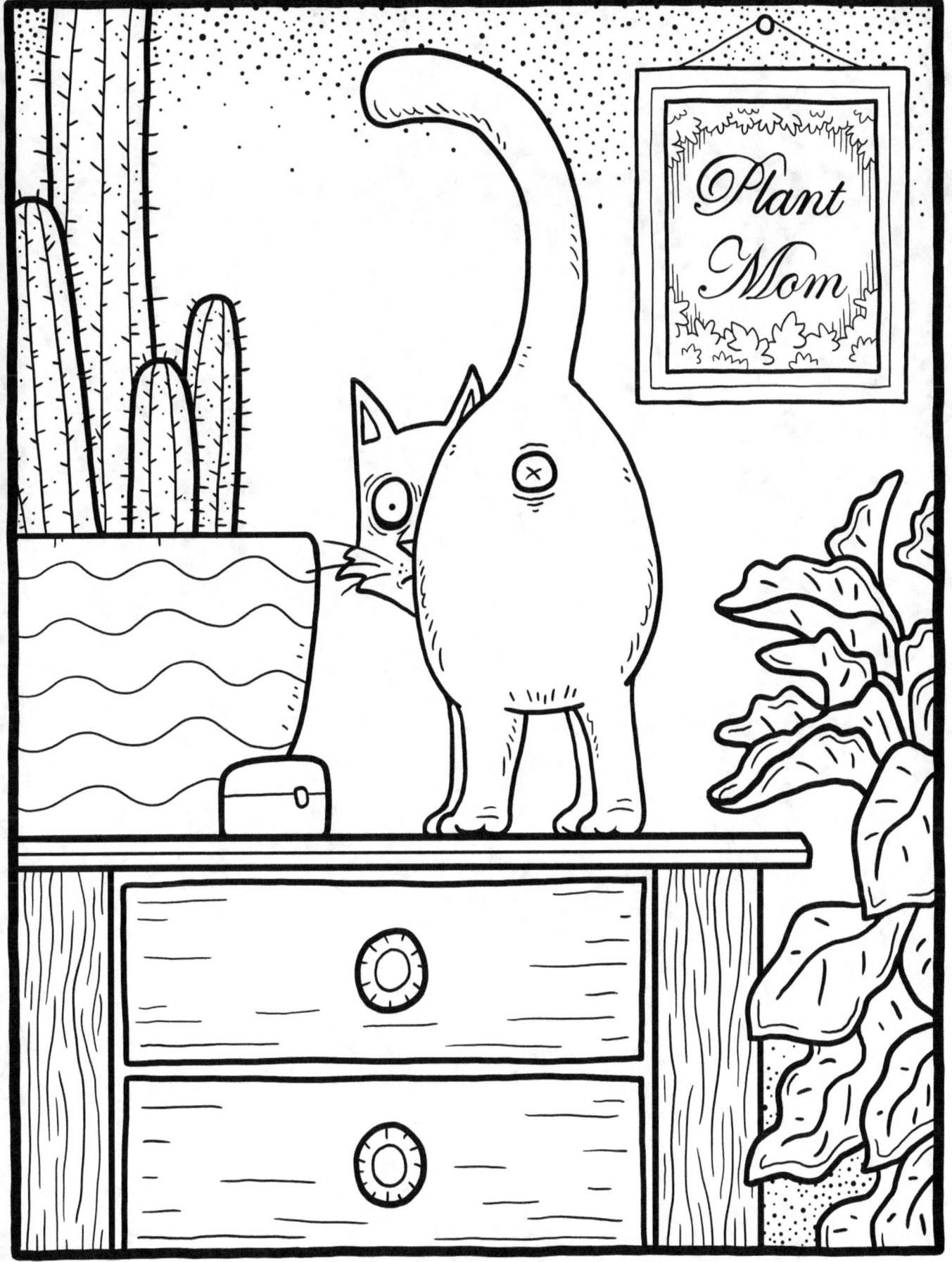

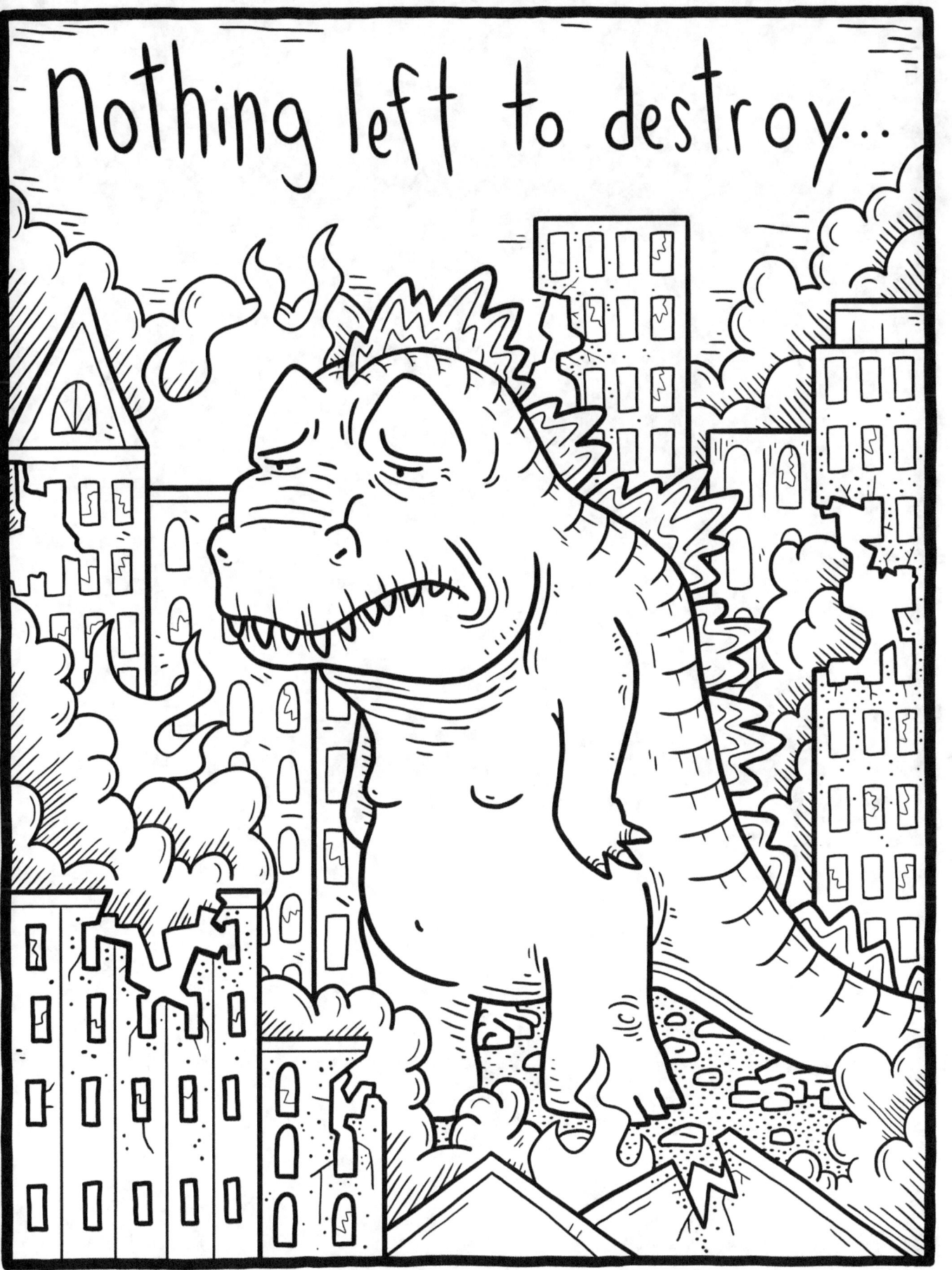

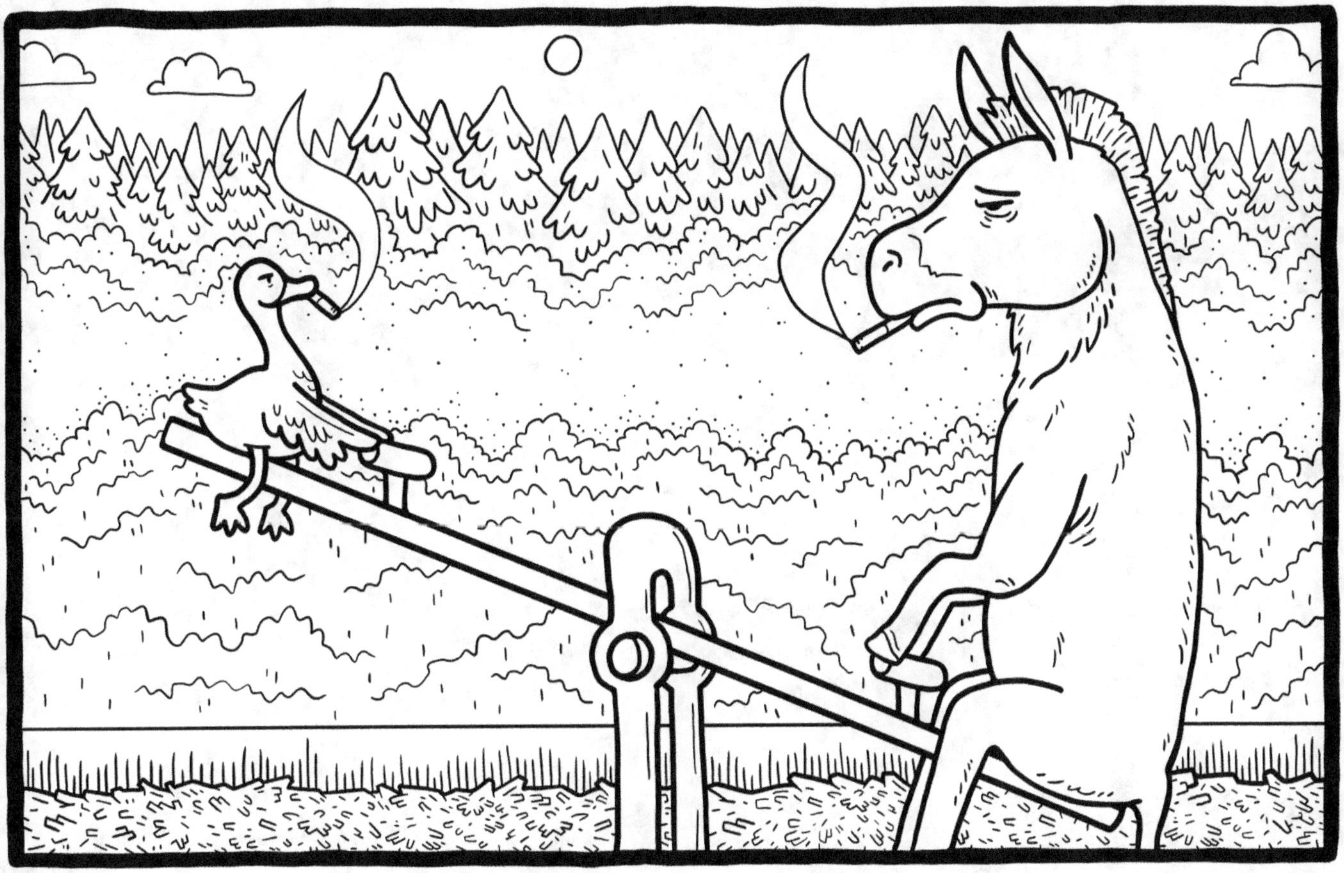

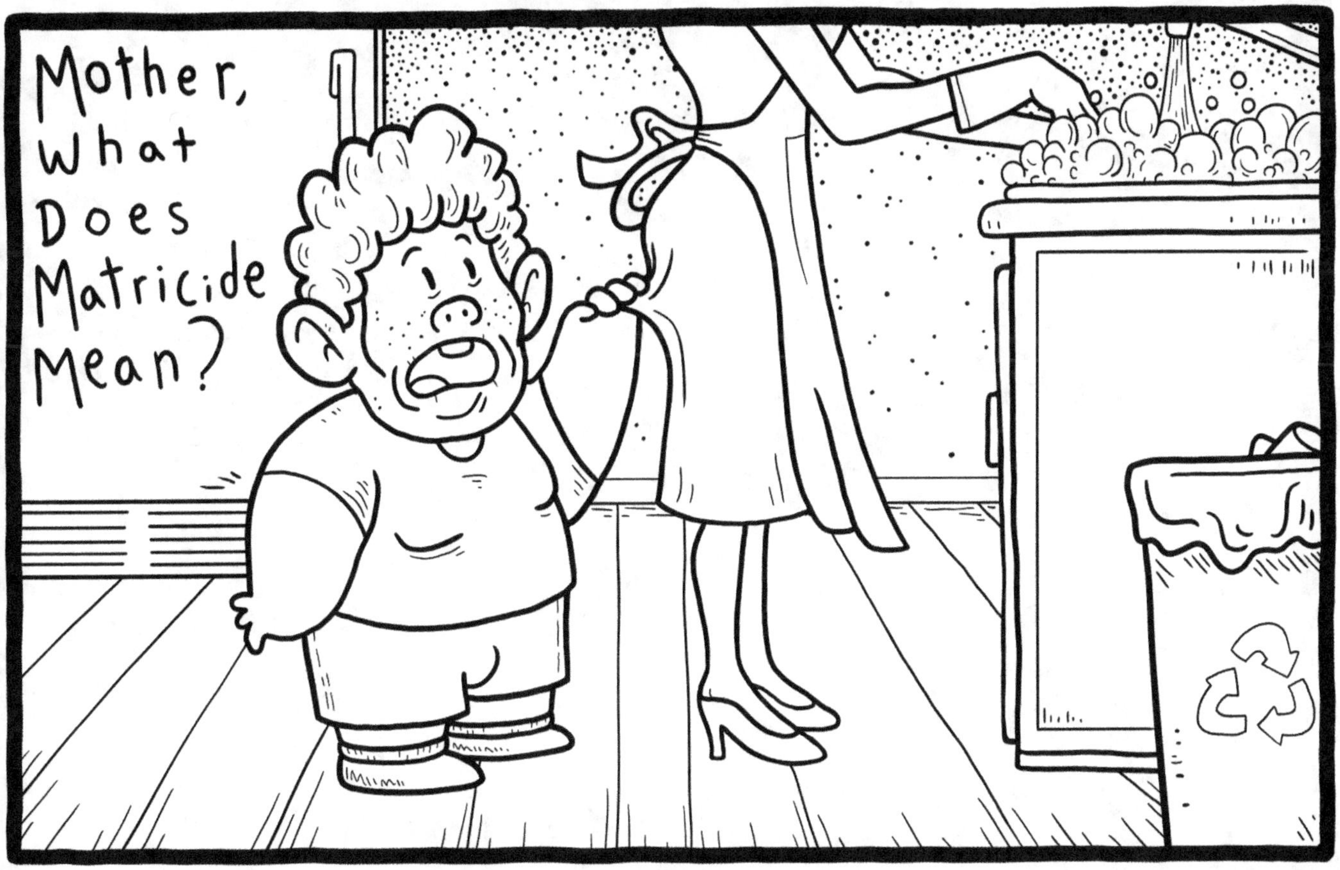

Mother, What Does Matricide Mean?

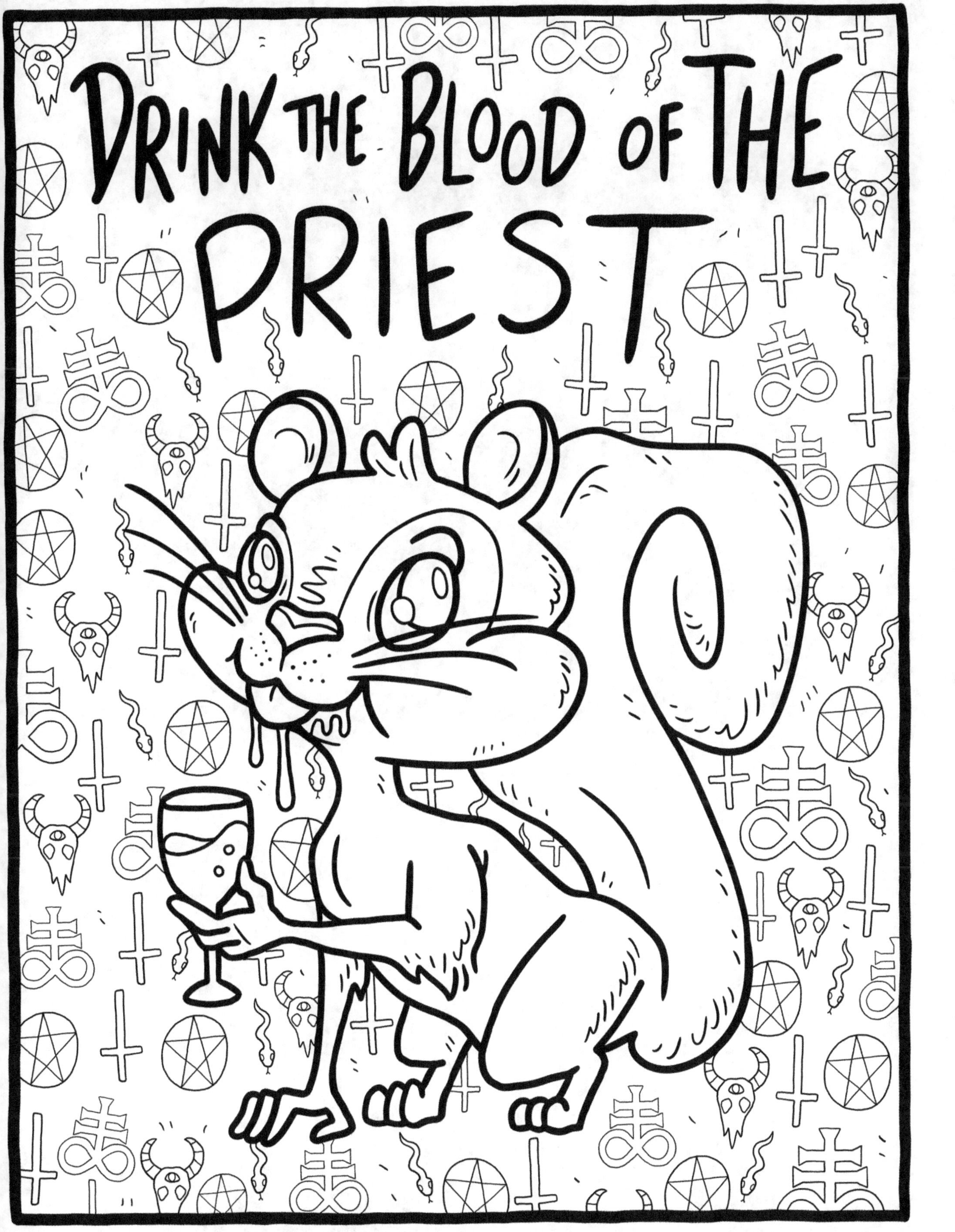

DRINK the Blood of THE PRIEST

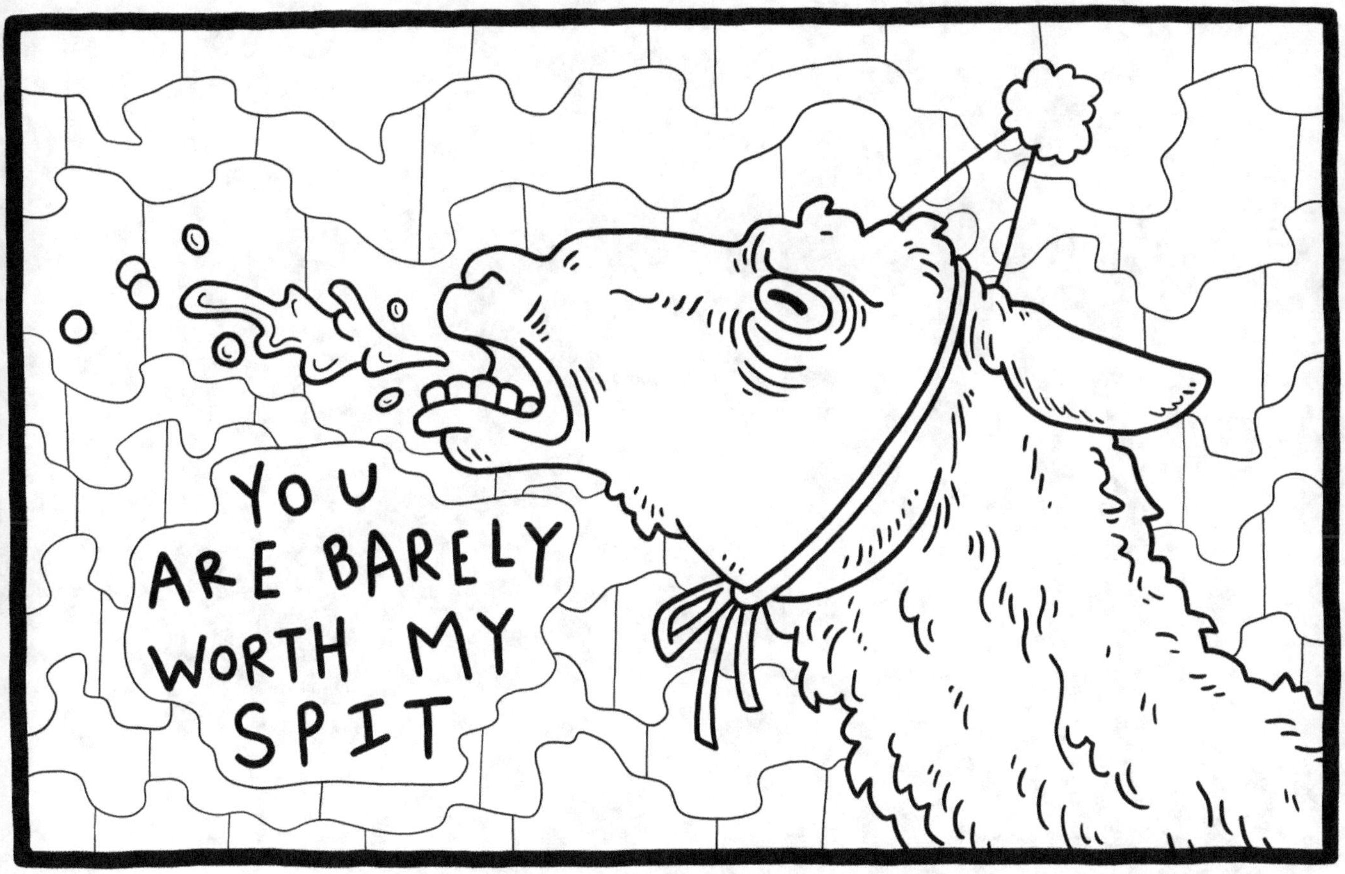

Panel 1: "YOU ARE BARELY WORTH MY SPIT"

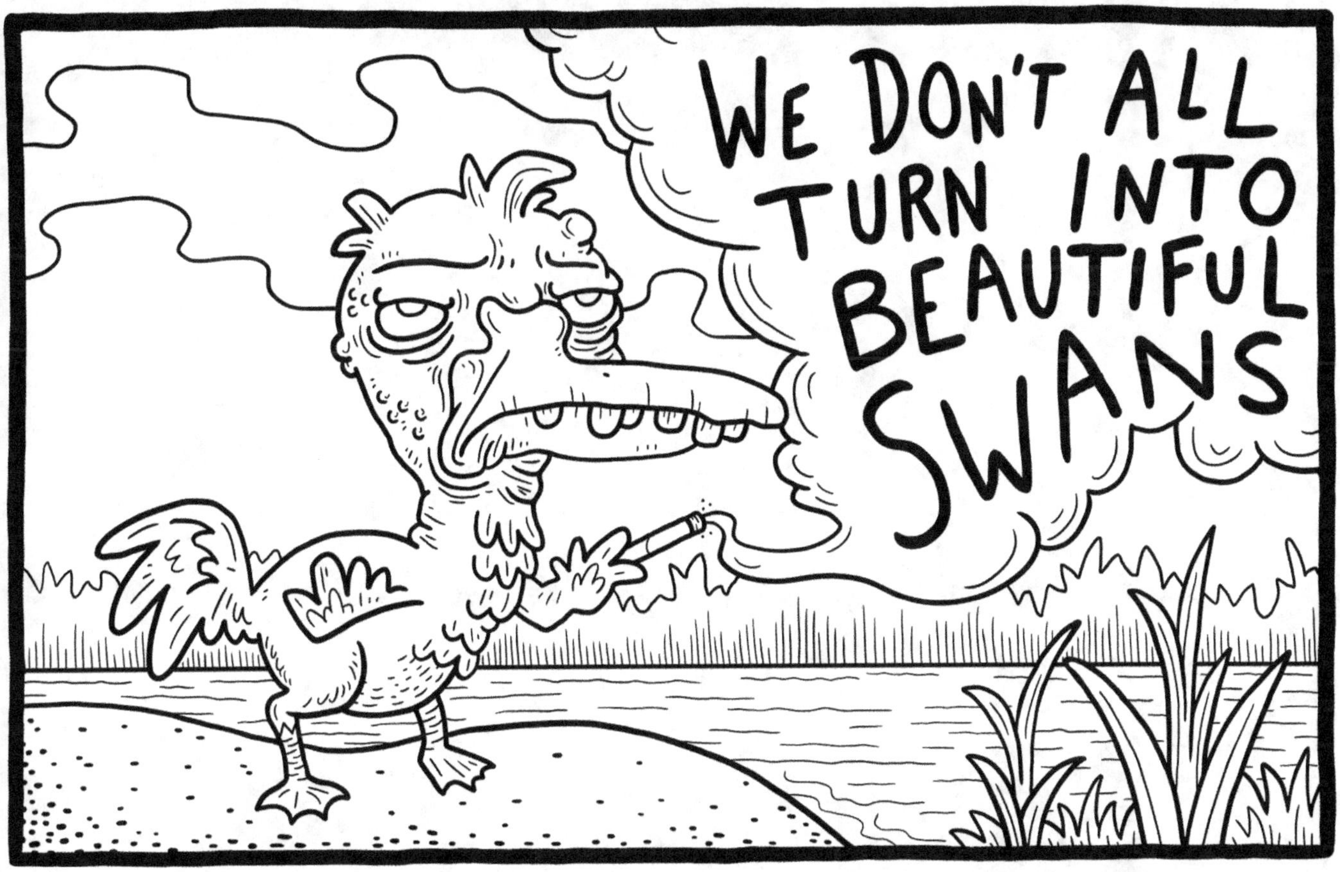

Panel 2: "WE DON'T ALL TURN INTO BEAUTIFUL SWANS"

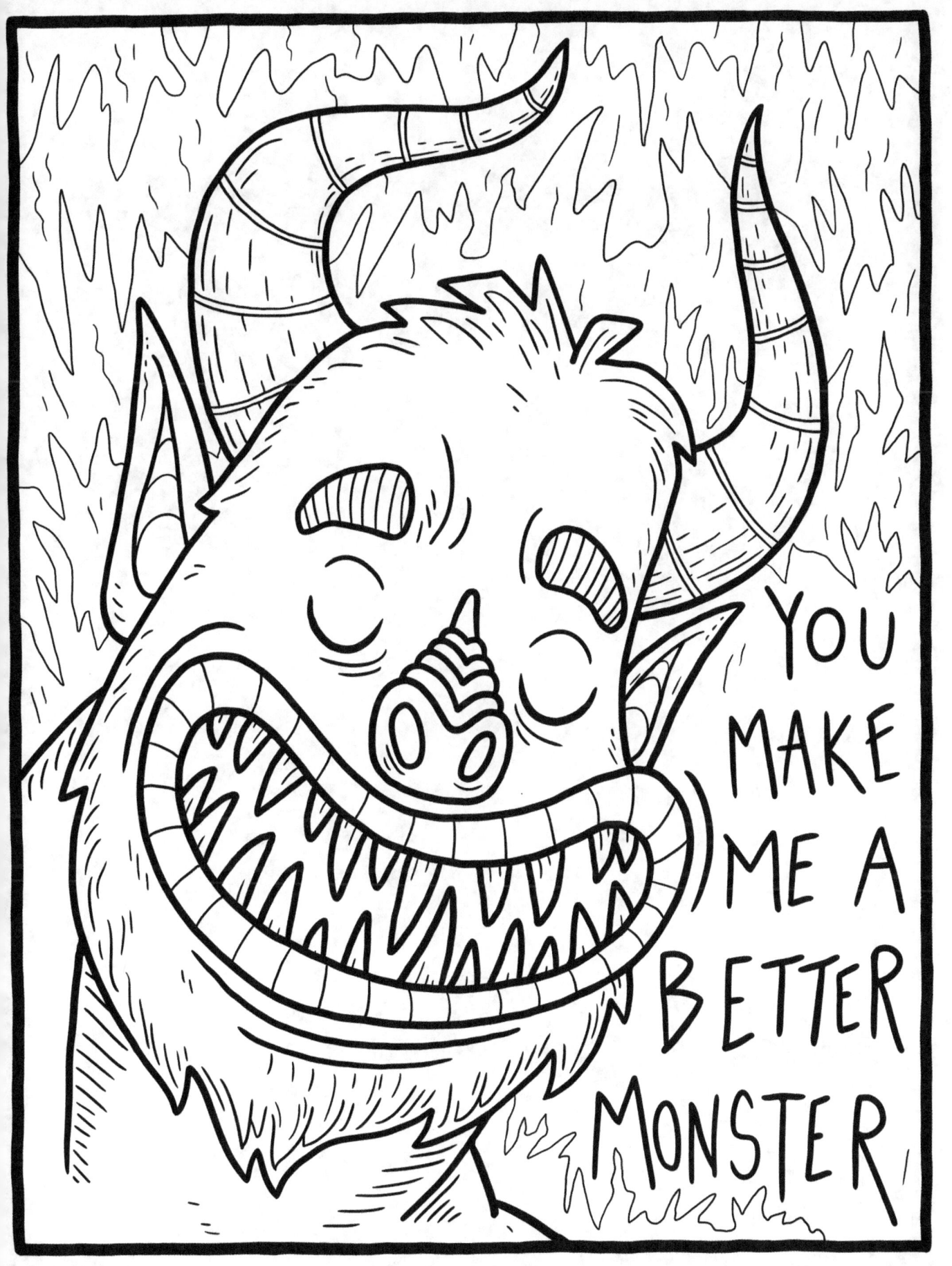

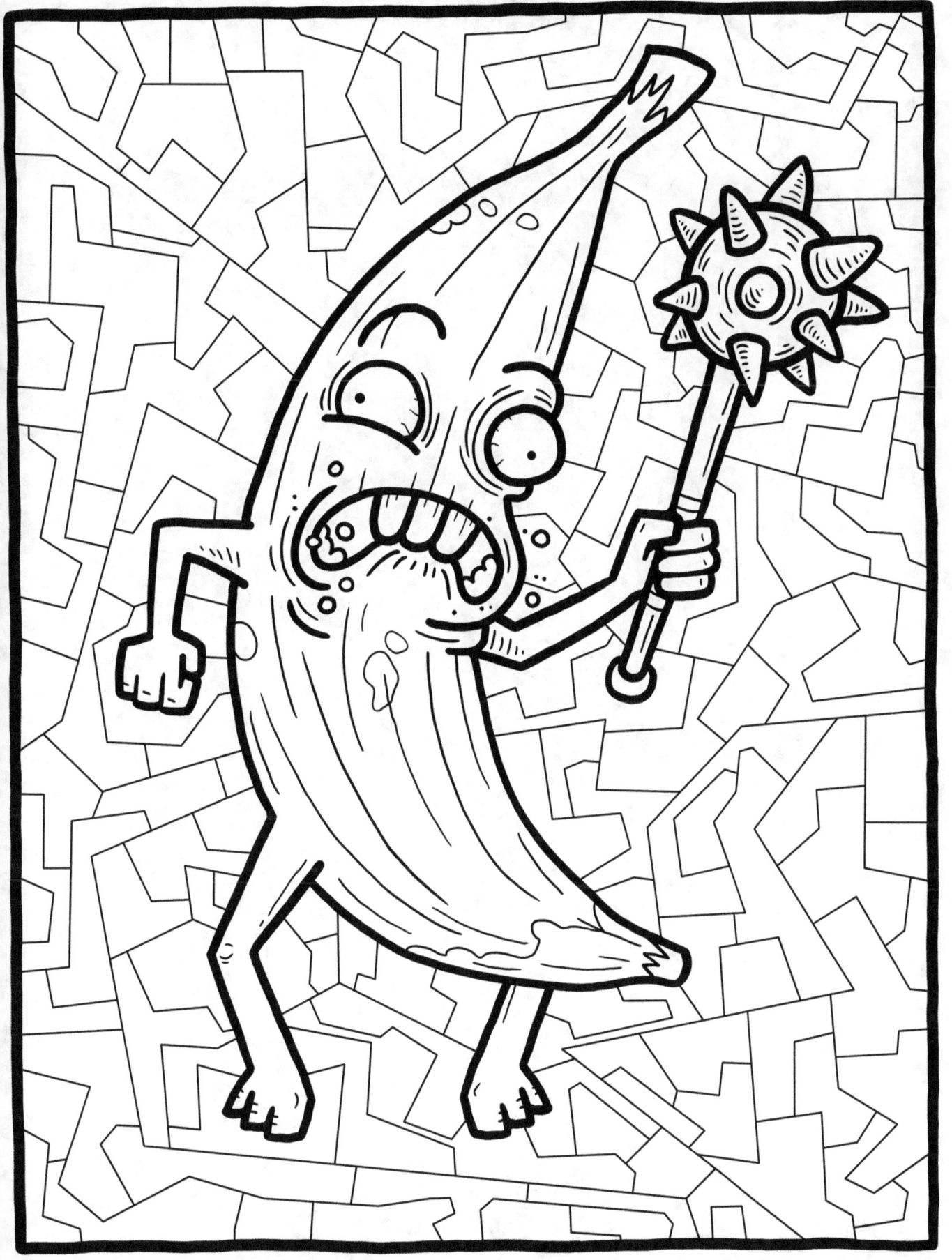

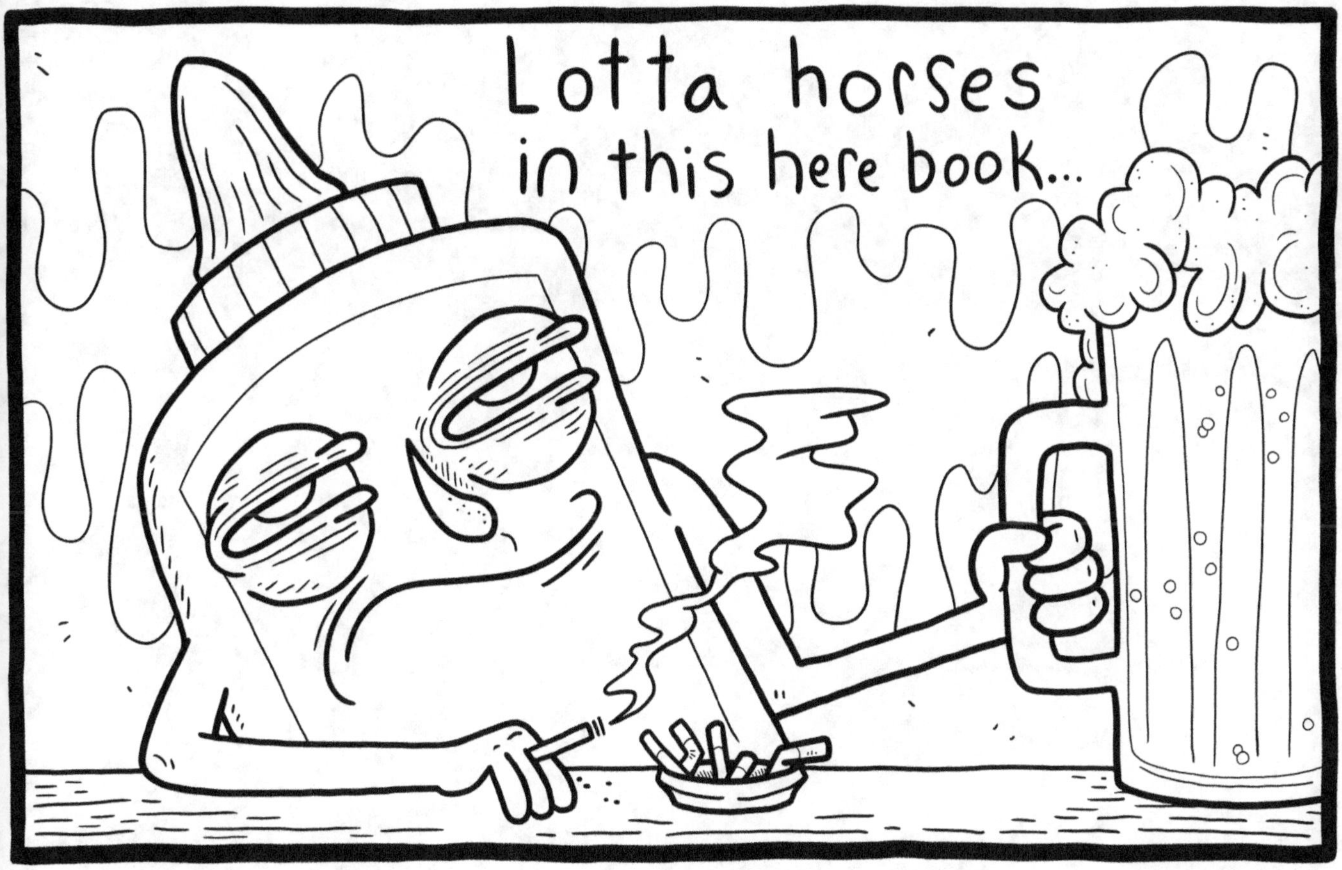

Lotta horses in this here book...

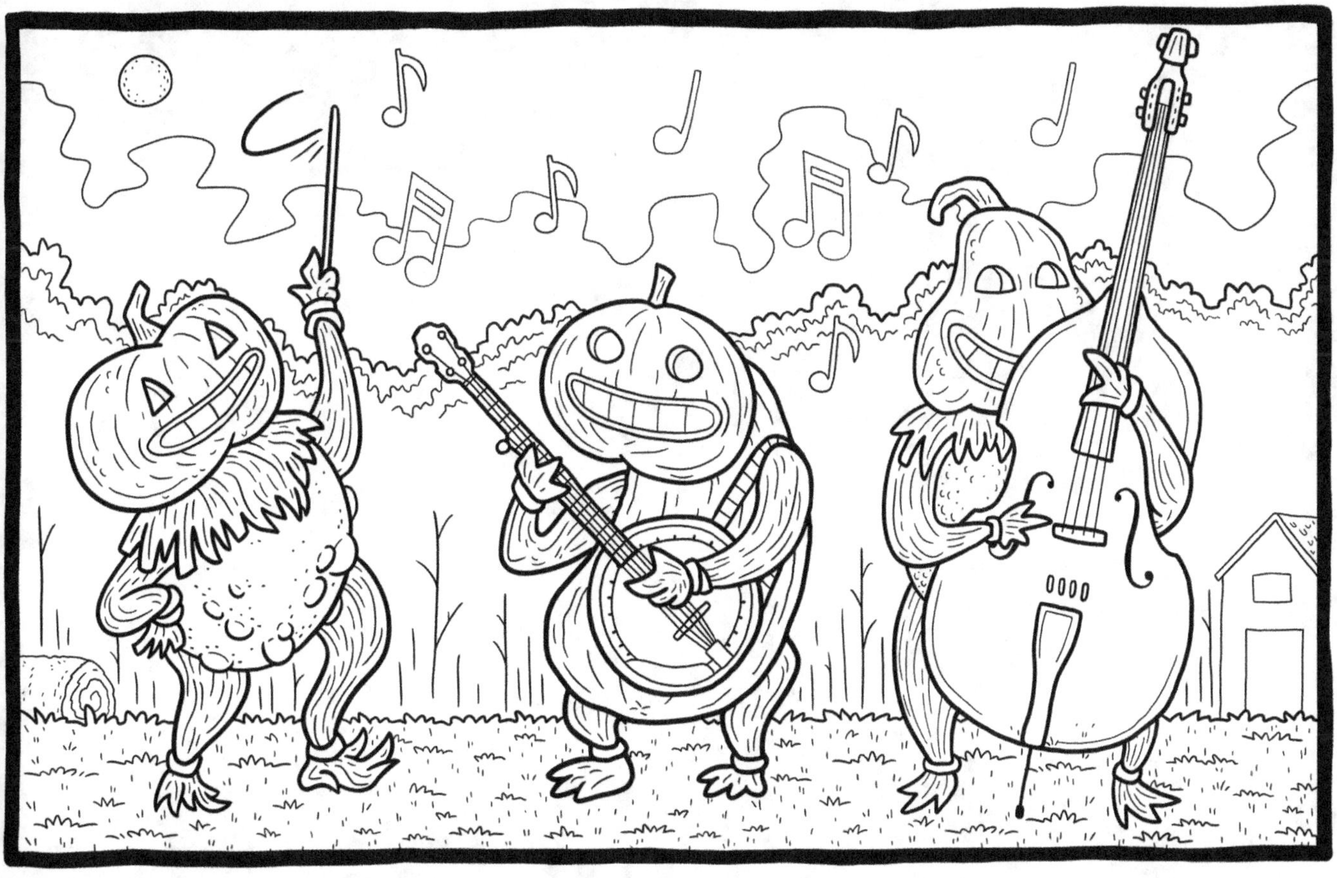

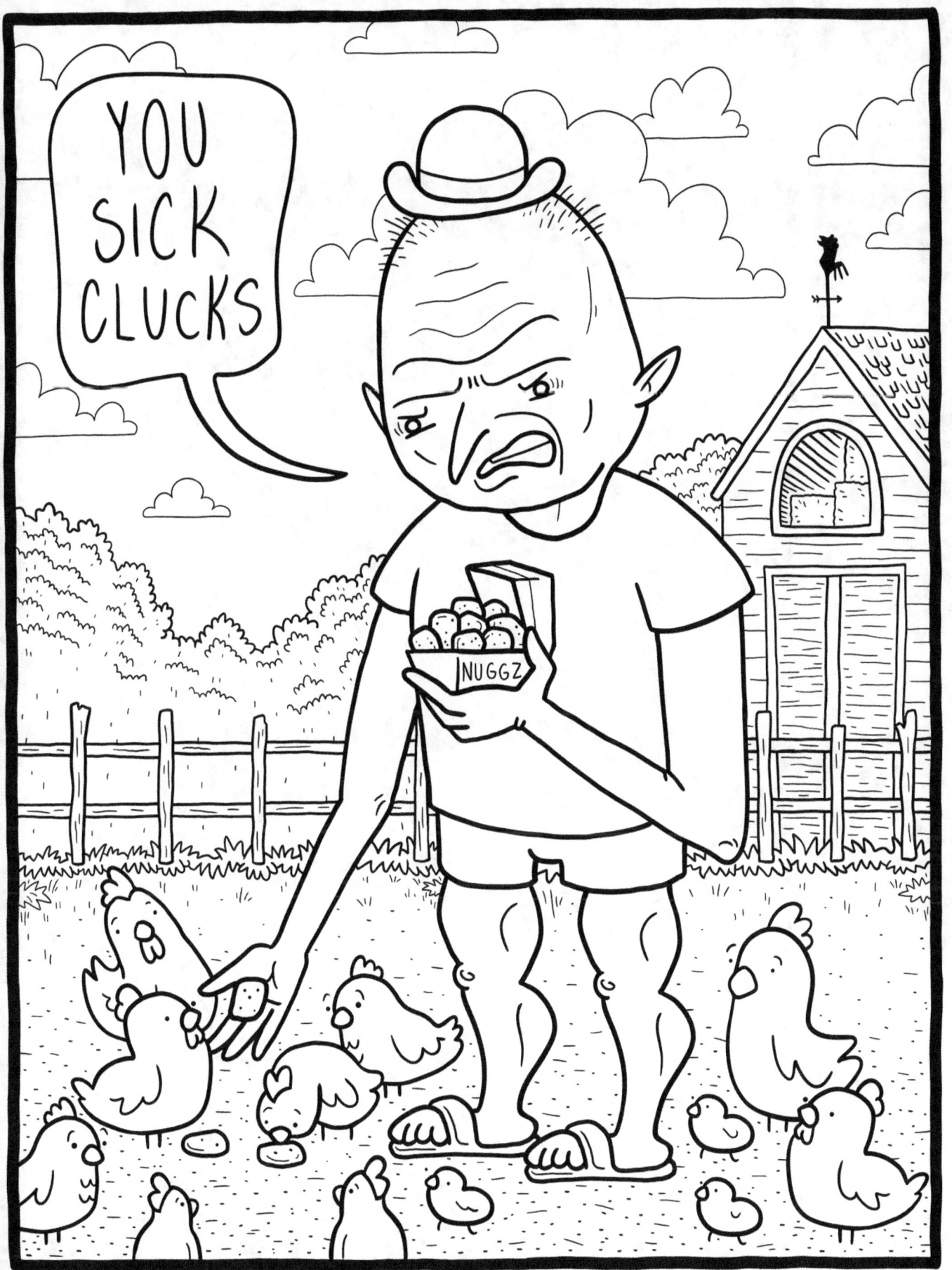

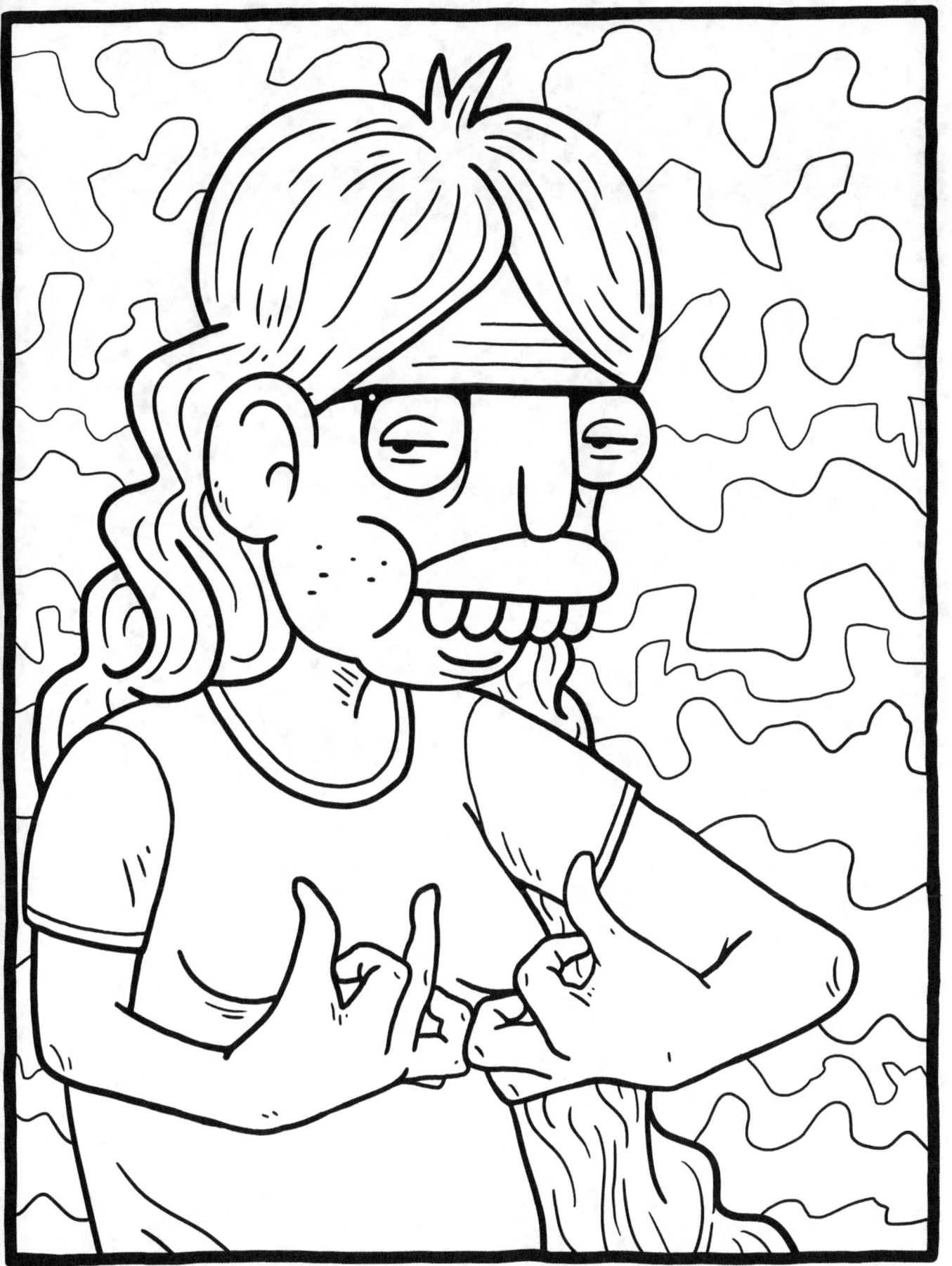

www.ingramcontent.com/pod-product-compliance
Lightning Source LLC
Chambersburg PA
CBHW060427220526
45465CB00008B/3044